"Fresh, innovative, and yet deeply rooted in biblical patterns of incarnational love. Paul challenges us through wisdom, not guilt, to be real. Can't wait to share this book with my Friday night small group!"
—JIM KILLGORE, president/CEO, ACMC

"This book is passionate, challenging, compassionate, convincing, and well-written. Paul Borthwick is one of the world's premiere authorities on sharing the faith. We should read *Stop Witnessing . . . and Start Loving* every year."
—JIM BURNS, PH.D., president, YouthBuilders

"Paul Borthwick takes us on a journey with a noble destination—reaching the least and the lost with the love of Jesus Christ. Authentic and transparent, this book emphasizes the importance of 'being' as opposed to simply 'doing.' Paul's kind of 'inside-out evangelism' is extremely clear and compelling."
—JOHN D. HULL, president, EQUIP, Atlanta, Georgia;
author of *Pivotal Praying*

"Grounded with a biblical foundation, Paul's refreshingly honest and realistic approach gives hope to the ordinary Christian making ordinary attempts to share Christ. I highly recommend *Stop Witnessing . . . and Start Loving* to those who have given up on sharing their faith because of past failure or because it seems too difficult."
—REVEREND RICHARD RHODES

STOP
WITNESSING
and START LOVING

Paul Borthwick

NAVPRESS

Bringing Truth to Life
P.O. Box 35001, Colorado Springs, Colorado 80935

OUR GUARANTEE TO YOU

We believe so strongly in the message of our books that we are making this quality guarantee to you. If for any reason you are disappointed with the content of this book, return the title page to us with your name and address and we will refund to you the list price of the book. To help us serve you better, please briefly describe why you were disappointed. Mail your refund request to: NavPress, P.O. Box 35002, Colorado Springs, CO 80935.

The Navigators is an international Christian organization. Our mission is to reach, disciple, and equip people to know Christ and to make Him known through successive generations. We envision multitudes of diverse people in the United States and every other nation who have a passionate love for Christ, live a lifestyle of sharing Christ's love, and multiply spiritual laborers among those without Christ.

NavPress is the publishing ministry of The Navigators. NavPress publications help believers learn biblical truth and apply what they learn to their lives and ministries. Our mission is to stimulate spiritual formation among our readers.

ISBN 1-57683-233-3

Cover design by Dan Jamison
Cover photo by PhotoSpin
Creative Team: Don Simpson, Brad Lewis, Nat Akin, Laura Spray, Glynese Northam

Some of the anecdotal illustrations in this book are true to life and are included with the permission of the persons involved. All other illustrations are composites of real situations, and any resemblance to people living or dead is coincidental.

Unless otherwise identified, all Scripture quotations in this publication are taken from the HOLY BIBLE: NEW INTERNATIONAL VERSION® (NIV®). Copyright © 1973, 1978, 1984 by International Bible Society. Used by permission of Zondervan Publishing House. All rights reserved. Other versions used include: the *New American Standard Bible* (NASB), © The Lockman Foundation 1960, 1962, 1963, 1968, 1971, 1972, 1973, 1975, 1977; *The Message: New Testament with Psalms and Proverbs* by Eugene H. Peterson, copyright © 1993, 1994, 1995, used by permission of NavPress Publishing Group; *The Holy Bible, New Century Version* copyright © 1987, 1988, 1991 by Word Publishing, Dallas, Texas 75039. Used by permission; and the *King James Version* (KJV).

Borthwick, Paul, 1954-
    Stop witnessing, and start loving / Paul Borthwick.
        p. cm.
Includes bibliographical references.
    ISBN 1-57683-233-3
    1. Witness bearing (Christianity) I. Title.
    BV4520 .B59 2003
    248'.5--dc21
                                    2002015678

Printed in the United States of America

1 2 3 4 5 6 7 8 9 10 / 07 06 05 04 03

DEDICATION

I begin this book with a deep sense of appreciation. I'm thankful to the kind editors at NavPress. They not only dedicated hours to improve my writing and make this book more readable, they also kindly granted me grace as I completed it.

I'm thankful for my friends who encouraged and, in some cases, inspired, the completion of this book—Richard Rhodes, Steve Macchia, the guys in our men's small group, and our prayer supporters.

Most of all, however, I thank God for Christie—my best friend, life partner, and wife. Her heart for the lost, especially expressed through her prayers and her diligence in lifestyle witness, have inspired me to persevere. I gladly dedicate this book to her.

TABLE OF CONTENTS

FOREWORD

Why is it when we lose something very precious to us that we frantically muster up every ounce of available energy to find it once again?

While speaking at a conference recently, one of the attendees shared with me that his 15-year-old granddaughter had been missing for nearly 24 hours. He was uncertain if he would be staying at the conference since his mind was so distracted with this news, and all he wanted to do was leave immediately, drive 250 miles to his daughter's home, and participate in the search.

I assured my new friend that he would be missed, but that everyone present would certainly understand his compelling reason for leaving. He was in tears as I prayed for his broken heart, his family, and most specifically, for his lost granddaughter. I was drawn into his pain as a father, remained prayerful in his behalf as a concerned brother in Christ, invited others to pray for the lost child, and anticipated all the potential heart-wrenching options if she were not found.

Within a few hours, this gentleman entered our seminar room and with gleeful exuberance interrupted my teaching with an enthusiastic "thumbs up"—the lost had been found! We all rejoiced together with great sighs of relief, offered a prayer of gratitude to God, and celebrated with this jubilant granddaddy. The all-out search for a precious lost soul had been successful, and the family of God gave thanks.

Why is it, on the other hand, when we know there are spiritually "lost" people scattered across the globe—and even across the street— that we don't muster up every available ounce of Spirit-empowered energy within us to reach them (no matter the cost) with the life-changing gospel message of love in Jesus Christ? For the committed believer, this is the heart of the matter.

God's heart is for the lost. And, his heart can be reproduced within us. Paul Borthwick, my long-time friend and accountability partner, offers us a thorough understanding of why lost people matter so much to Almighty God and, frankly, why they should matter to us! Through bibically sound teachings and examples that speak clearly of God's heart, Borthwick provides for the reader a healthy theology of evangelism. This theology is plentifully illustrated with practical, relational application.

When you discover a book with passion, zeal, excitement, boldness, and overflowing heartfelt witness, you want to read it cover to cover. This is one such book, especially when the author is unashamed to call lost people lost—as Jesus himself calls them—without concern for being politically correct. I know from firsthand experience that what Paul Borthwick writes is from the depth of personal convictions that have been borne out of anguish over the lostness of those he loves. His concern is not for political correctness—it's for missional effectiveness.

As one who has been rescued out of darkness, my friend and brother in Christ is compelled by the gospel to reach out to others with the love of Jesus. As a result, he has seen incredible victory as well as disappointing heartache. He writes to all of his readers out of his own earnest desire to infiltrate his world as a powerful witness for Christ. Because of the urgent need to reach the lost, he calls us out of our lethargy and urges us to become conspicuous Christian witnesses in a dark and needy world. Get ready for the challenge. Borthwick pulls out all the stops and doesn't hold back!

Does it matter to you that lost people are heading to eternal damnation if they are not reached with the gospel? If so, then rekindle the fire within you and rebuke your excuses for avoiding evangelistic "divine appointments." With gratitude of heart, respond to his call, serve as a catalyst for his grace, and watch how God's transforming hope comes alive through you to love the lost within your reach!

"The light that shines the furthest shines brightest close to home." May it be so for you!

Stephen A. Macchia, D.Min.

President, Vision New England

Author, *Becoming a Healthy Church*

DRY BONES OR
CONTAGIOUS CHRISTIANS?

A heart for lost people can change your life!

Before I read the book *How to Be a Contagious Christian* by Bill Hybels and Mark Mittelburg, I loved the title. I said, "Yes, Lord, that's what I want to be—a contagious Christian." I want my life to spread the love of God like a positive, hope-filled virus that can spiritually infect other people for the better.

Don't you?

The apostle Paul wrote to the Romans about being eager to preach Jesus Christ to lost people. I read that verse and I echo the prayer, "Yes, Lord, that's what I want to be—eager to preach Christ, enthusiastic about my faith, and overflowing with the joy of being forgiven." I want to be good advertising for new life in Christ.

Don't you?

But when I do some self-evaluation, I find flaws and shortcomings as a witness for Jesus in my daily life. Rather than being an effervescent, overflowing Christian, I find myself prone to spiritual deadness. I'm like the people of Israel that Ezekiel called "dry bones." Rather than being a contagious Christian in society, spreading the love of Christ like a virus of hope, I find myself more like the spiritually self-satisfied people in the church of Laodicea whom Jesus called "lukewarm."

I think I'm not alone. Many followers of Christ feel like failures as witnesses. We belong to the people of God, but our lives testify to an apathy, complacency, or boredom about the faith.

Consider the various ways we refer to ourselves in the church. Technically, the term *Christian* should be able to stand alone without adjectives. It means a follower of Christ, an imitator of Christ, one who belongs to Christ. But, over the centuries of Christianity, we've added a host of adjectives. These include positive phrases like "born-again," "charismatic," or "Bible-believing" Christian.

But we also include negative phrases like "nominal," "backslidden," or "carnal." Most of us would agree that adding adjectives to create combinations like bored Christian, nominal Christian, lukewarm Christian, or apathetic Christian should be oxymoronic—opposites that are mutually exclusive—when referring to devotees of the Lord Jesus.

Then we go to church. There we find it easy to know everything about doctrine, all the while ignoring the needy. Would Jesus compare us to "whitewashed tombs" (Matthew 23:27)?

We might come from the family who started the church, and we might enjoy power and influence in church politics, but if we never witness to the love of Christ to those outside the faith, would Paul describe us as a person "having a form of godliness but denying its power" (2 Timothy 3:5)?

Some of us have experience as veterans of service on a thousand committees, but our spiritual lives are dull. Would Ezekiel call us "dry bones" (see Ezekiel 37:1-11)?

Maybe the last time we actually led someone else to Jesus Christ was twenty years ago. Now we seldom speak of our faith at work or in the community. Would Jesus identify us as "lukewarm" (Revelation 3:16)?

When we examine our own spiritual vitality, especially as it pertains to our love and zeal for outreach to lost people, we fall short. We're preoccupied with peripheral issues. We're distracted from reaching out to others. We grow cold in our faith. And we fail to present to our nonreligious friends the abundant life Christ promises.

So, how do we resurrect our desire to be contagious Christians? How do we get excited again about following Jesus Christ and sharing his love with others? What will reignite an eagerness to tell others about God's love? In other words, how do we regain our heart for the lost?

WHAT THIS BOOK IS ABOUT

If you picked this book up to learn 101 new techniques for witnessing, you'll be disappointed. If you're looking for a new resource on how to answer difficult questions from those outside the Christian faith, sorry, this isn't it.

This book isn't about technique or apologetics. It's about heart. It's about our basic desires, motivations, and perspectives as Christians in contemporary society. It's about the "what makes me tick?"–type questions of life.

A couple of years ago, my supervisor at church took a group of staff to Willow Creek Community Church in Illinois—one of the largest and most famous churches in North America. I went against my will—I already had strong opinions about the strengths and weaknesses of this church, so I objected with a don't-confuse-me-with-the-facts resistance. But that conference changed my life. An excellent program, fine materials, and more content than I could digest in a year. But that's not what changed me.

My life was changed because the speakers helped me regain my heart for lost people. It wasn't through some seminar or how-to talk. It emanated from their lives. They told stories about winning people to Christ—and none of the stories were more than six months old. They prioritized outreach to others in spite of the busyness of church schedules and demands.

When they talked about people who hadn't come to faith in Christ, they wept. I could tell these leaders ached to see others come to new life and forgiveness in Christ.

My life changed because they exemplified Christians living with a heart for the lost. Their example became a wake-up call for me. Two months after this reawakening of my own heart for the lost, I left the security of twenty-two years of employment in order to dedicate myself more fully to serving lost people.

WHAT ABOUT YOU?

At this point, you might be thinking you'll just put down this book. You're thinking to yourself, *I'm not sure I'm ready to upset my life quite that much to rebuild a heart for lost people.*

I can't promise you that this book will do for you what the seminar at Willow Creek did for me. But I can promise you this: It will challenge you. I hope it will challenge you to renew your passion to know Jesus Christ. I hope it will stir you to look at people around you with a fresh, biblical vision. And I pray that I can encourage or challenge your understanding of yourself as God's agent for change in this broken world.

And if God uses something I share in these pages to rekindle your heart for lost people—even to the point of leaving twenty-two years or more of security so you can serve lost people—I'd love to hear about it.

Paul Borthwick
Lexington, Massachusetts

HEART BUILDER #1:

REKINDLE
YOUR PASSION

Passion for outreach is not
our first priority.

You might think that a book like this would start with a call to be zealous to reach out to those outside of the Christian faith. But zeal for outreach is not the starting point. Passion is. Your core passion. The thing that gets you up and keeps you going. The thing—when you confront it—that causes you to conclude, "Yes. This is what I'm living for!"

So . . . what's *your* passion?

Social observers say that we live in a passionless age. Observers of our pluralistic culture conclude that our main value seems to be total acceptance of everything and commitment to nothing, even referring to the early twenty-first century as the "age of indifferentism."

The editors of *Leadership* magazine captured this in a cartoon. A pastor is speaking to a group of adults—obviously calling them to a life of higher commitment and discipleship. A fellow in the back raises his hand and asks, "Pastor, is it possible to *audit* this class on total commitment?"

We live in a culture of halfheartedness. We fear passion because we're against obsessive-compulsive behaviors. Yet ironically, every weekend, millions of Americans will sit and watch sports figures passionately battle it out! And passionate fans scream, color their faces, and brave extreme weather in order to support their favorite athletes. We've developed the ability to be passionate about things that don't matter eternally while being apathetic about the true meaning of life.

WHAT IS PASSION?

Before exploring *how* we might rekindle our passion—either for Christ or for lost people—we need to understand what passion looks like. One dictionary defines passion as "fervor, enthusiasm, zeal, an intense emotion compelling action."[1]

The biblical word for passion takes it a step further. The Greek word *pascho* literally is linked to the verb meaning "to suffer," translated as "[Christ's] suffering" (Acts 1:3). If you're from a liturgical background, you understand this connection; the week between Palm Sunday and Easter is Passion Week—the week of the suffering, torture, and crucifixion of Jesus Christ.

Combine the dictionary definition with the biblical meaning related to suffering, and we come up with a fuller understanding of passion:

Passion is something we're so intensely committed to that we'd be willing to suffer or die for it.

So, I need to warn you up front: there's no such thing as pain-free passion. There's no passion-lite, no partial or halfhearted passion.

Passionate people pay the price, absorb the cost, and go after their purposes with sold-out zeal.

John Henry Jowett, a British pastor of a century ago, described a life of passion when he exhorted people to live life to God's fullest and to avoid stagnation:

> It is possible to evade a multitude of sorrows through the cultivation of an insignificant life. Indeed, if a person's ambition is to avoid the troubles of life, the recipe is simple: shed your ambitions in every direction, cut the wings of every soaring purpose, and seek a life with the fewest contacts and relations. If you want to get through life with the smallest trouble, you must reduce yourself to the smallest compass. Tiny souls can dodge through life; bigger souls are blocked on every side. As soon as a person begins to enlarge his or her life, resistances are multiplied. Let a person remove petty selfish purposes and enthrone Christ, and sufferings will be increased on every side.[2]

IMAGES OF PASSION

It helps us understand passion when we see images of passion.

The cover story of an April 1997 issue of *Sports Illustrated* featured an exposé of drug use in sports.[3] To set the tone, the writers surveyed 196 Olympic athletes and asked, "If you knew you would not be caught, would you be willing to take performance-enhancing drugs or steroids if you knew that they enable you to win a gold medal?"

Guess how many said they'd take these drugs if they knew they'd win and wouldn't get caught? One hundred ninety-two of 196 (97.9 percent)! Their zeal to win obviously suppressed any ethical or moral issues that could have stopped them from cheating.

The second question, however, really illustrated the passion that these Olympians had to win a gold medal. The *Sports Illustrated* reporters asked,

"If you knew that you could win a gold medal, and wouldn't be caught—but you would die in five years—would you still take these drugs?"

More than 100 of the 196 (51 percent) surveyed said that they would still take the drugs—even if they'd die in five years! Sound warped? I suppose so, but passion never looks normal to the passionless. We might think these athletes have lost all perspective on their lives and sports—but they provide a powerful picture of the sacrifices people will make when they're passionate about a higher goal.

A second picture of passion comes from a June 1994 *National Geographic* article entitled "King of Fibers."[4] The feature article didn't intrigue me at all, but a sidebar describing the ordeals the author and photographer endured in order to present the article did. For this story (that most of us would find a tough topic to get passionate about), the author and photographer:

- Made 160 contacts for interviews.
- Researched 65 books.
- Traveled to eleven countries.
- Carried fifteen tons of equipment in 171 crates, including a lab, a boat, and other machines.
- Suffered relationally (one of the contributors got divorced), personally (they were jailed, beaten, and robbed), and physically (suffering both malaria and dysentery) as the article was completed.
- Racked up hardships parallel to Paul's lists (in 2 Corinthians 6 and 11) of his own turmoil in preaching the gospel.

They went through this for one article and about seven photos that were published—on a relatively boring topic such as cotton. But they were passionate to get published, so they paid the price.

Young lovers who promise to "climb the highest mountain and swim the deepest sea" understand passion. A professional athlete who has a dislocated finger amputated so that he can play in the big game understands passion. One computer company's slogan summarizes their stated passion to satisfy their customers: "Whatever it takes!" Whatever it takes to reach the goal, to accomplish the mission, to complete the race. That's passion.

After my wife and I gave up years of job security to pursue what we understood as God's purposes for us, a young woman at our church wanted to affirm our passion to serve Christ. She came to us and stated simply, "Go crazy for God." She understood a whatever-it-takes passion.

Bill and Judy love Jesus Christ. Their lives testify to their passion to make that relationship the top priority of their lives. Their passion has led to bold and sometimes outrageous witness for Jesus—especially focusing on international visitors in their community from the Peoples Republic of China. They go on prayer walks around town on Saturday morning asking God to guide them to Chinese visitors. In the winter, they move their outreach indoors to the Chinese-foods section of the local supermarket. On any given Sunday, you'll find Bill and Judy sitting in church with two or three Chinese communist visitors they've met over the weekend—visitors who are hearing the good news about Jesus for the first time. Bill and Judy's outreach flows out of their love for Jesus Christ, and that love overflows to the people they touch.

Fred retired several years ago, but now—at age seventy and beyond—he dedicates every summer to short-term mission service, teaching English and reaching out to people in a country closed to missionaries. Fred's friends think he's crazy. He is! He's passionate about his relationship with Jesus Christ, and he wants to make Jesus known—whatever it takes.

A BIBLICAL PICTURE OF PASSION

When we think of godly passion—the type we want to rekindle so that we renew our heart for the lost—the picture to consider comes from

Paul in his letter to the Philippians. Writing from prison, Paul articulates his passion.

> But whatever was to my profit I now consider loss for the sake of Christ. What is more, I consider everything a loss compared to the surpassing greatness of knowing Christ Jesus my Lord, for whose sake I have lost all things. I consider them rubbish, that I may gain Christ and be found in him, not having a righteousness of my own that comes from the law, but that which is through faith in Christ—the righteousness that comes from God and is by faith. I want to know Christ and the power of his resurrection and the fellowship of sharing in his sufferings, becoming like him in his death, and so, somehow, to attain to the resurrection from the dead.
>
> Not that I have already obtained all this, or have already been made perfect, but I press on to take hold of that for which Christ Jesus took hold of me. Brothers, I do not consider myself yet to have taken hold of it. But one thing I do: Forgetting what is behind and straining toward what is ahead, I press on toward the goal to win the prize for which God has called me heavenward in Christ Jesus. (Philippians 3:7-14)

Paul, the great evangelist and apostle, serves as an obvious example of someone who lived with a heart for the lost people of his world. Here he articulates his supreme passion—to know Jesus Christ in both his power and his sufferings.

FIRST THINGS FIRST

A book on developing a heart for lost people obviously flows from the idea of passion, and you might think that the starting point is a passion to reach lost people. But the apostle Paul describes a different set of priorities. We don't start by building our passion to reach out to lost people. The sheer volume of people in need and resistance to the good news about Jesus will overwhelm us. We'll lose our passion either because the need is too immense or because the risk seems too large.

We also don't start by building our passion for righteousness or holiness. If we begin there, our own sinfulness and lack of progress will discourage us. Instead, we start by renewing our passion to know Christ.

Philippians 3:7-14 stands as a unique proclamation of Paul concerning his passion. He most likely writes this letter from a prison cell (see the references to chains in Philippians 1:7 and 1:13), and he sets this portion of the letter apart for his readers and for us with some unique vocabulary. He uses five specific Greek words that, in the entire Bible, appear only here in chapter 3:

- "rubbish" or *refuse* (verse 8)
- "becoming like him" or *conformed* (verse 10)
- "resurrection" (verse 11)
- "straining" (verse 13)
- "goal" (verse 14)

Why the unique language? Because Paul wants his readers to sit up and take notice. He's saying something special here. He's articulating his life passion—*namely, to know Jesus Christ!*

Remember, Paul is writing from prison. His pain and suffering help him focus on what he really believes in. When he uses the very strong word *rubbish*, he's telling his readers that all of his former passions (see Philippians 3:4-6) are nothing—rubbish, trash, dung, manure—compared to the surpassing value of knowing Christ.

When he says that he's "forgetting what is behind," he means, "I'm not resting on past laurels, past experiences, past loves." Instead, he's now "straining" for what lies ahead, like a competitive runner lunging across the finish line.

Paul's example confronts our passion. What are we passionate about? Am I passionate to know Christ and to make that the top priority of my life? Am I like Bunyan's pilgrim in *Pilgrim's Progress*, who, when lured by the securities and comforts of a passionless life, put his fingers in his ears and embarked on his journey, shouting, "Life, life, eternal life!"?[5] Am I passionate for eternal life—which is to know God and Jesus Christ, whom God sent (see John 17:3)?

Or have I grown cold and complacent, like those in the church at Ephesus in Revelation 2, who forgot their first love? Am I just interested in enough religion to season my life, like spice for my own self-centered existence?

Witness, evangelism, service—and all other forms of outreach—flow from a passion to know Christ. Out of that passion flows our love for lost people. When we're filled with the love of Christ and understand his love for us, then we overflow and touch the lives of the people around us.

REKINDLE THE PASSION

So the question becomes "How?" How can we rekindle a fire that burns with the desire to know Jesus Christ? How can we fuel the flame with passionate zeal to know Christ—a flame that makes all other pursuits seem like rubbish by comparison? Four exercises can help set us on the right path.

Exercise #1: Pray Psalm 86:11. The psalmist prays, "Give me an undivided heart, that I may fear your name." In other words, "Lord, I ask you to focus my life and help me stay focused on what is supposed to be my top priority."

I know how to quote Philippians 3:14—"one thing I do"—but I live a life that's scattered. Some days I'm zealous to know Christ, but other days a thousand other interests distract me. Most of these are not evil things. They're just less than the best thing, which is knowing

Christ. I pray Psalm 86:11: "Lord, I'm scattered, distracted, unfocused. Unite my heart. Bring all aspects of my life under the supreme target of knowing Jesus Christ."

When knowing Jesus is truly my top priority, then outreach, service, and evangelism come as natural by-products. When my life focus is diffused by any number of secondary priorities, top concerns like outreach, service, and evangelism get squeezed out of my schedule.

Exercise #2: Fuel the passion to know Christ by being with "passionate-to-know-God" people. I've had the privilege of knowing George Verwer, founder of Operation Mobilization, over the past few years. George fuels my passion to know Christ. His love for the world and his desire to see people come to know Christ flows from his relationship with Jesus Christ. When my heart grows cold, it always helps to read something George wrote, listen to one of his tapes, or—on a few unique occasions—pray with George personally.

If we want to catch fire with the zeal to know Christ, then we need to be with people who are on fire themselves. Their zeal can ignite us. We all do well to find a friend who helps fuel our fire to know Christ.

What do you do if no one like that is around? If no living person can help you refocus your commitment to know Jesus Christ, then go to the library and find some biographies of Christian heroes who've gone before us. Reading great stories of people like Jim Elliot, Amy Carmichael, C. T. Studd, or Hudson Taylor (to name only a few) can stir us to imitate their zeal to know Jesus Christ.

Exercise #3: Don't waste your pain. This third exercise designed to rekindle passion to know Christ comes right out of Philippians 3:10. Paul writes that he wants to "know Christ and the power of his resurrection and the fellowship of sharing in his sufferings." All of us want that first part—the power of Christ's resurrection. But few of us want the second—the fellowship of sharing in Christ's sufferings.

What's Paul saying here? Does he advocate a spiritual masochism where we go looking for opportunities to suffer? Of course not. He's merely stating a theme throughout the Bible—that God uses or allows hardship in our lives to draw us to himself, deepen our character, and intensify our witness.

In Psalm 119, the psalmist observes twice that suffering was good for him because it produced obedience (see Psalm 119:67,71). Paul tells Christians to rejoice in their sufferings because suffering produces perseverance, and perseverance produces character (see Romans 5:3). The writer of the book of Hebrews reminds us that God disciplines those he loves, and that even Jesus learned obedience through suffering (see Hebrews 5:8).

Are we willing to allow our disappointments and pains to foster our total dependence on God? Amy Carmichael, whose missionary career spanned more than fifty years, spent more than half those years confined to her sickbed. Yet it was her sufferings that led to many books and poems reflecting the depth of her character.

Growing through pain is never easy. Our human response to any type of pain—physical, emotional, or social—starts with the prayer, "Lord, please take away the pain." But what do we do when God doesn't take away the pain—at least in ways we would choose? Our second prayer should be, "Lord, if you're not going to take away this pain, then please use it to fuel my desire to know you."

It's not easy to stay passionate through our pain. Several years ago, after rupturing a disk in my lower back, I was living with greater physical pain than I'd ever experienced before. I couldn't sleep, sit, or stand without constant discomfort. As a reflection of my own "deep spirituality," I remember praying: "Lord, if you want to use this pain to make me more Christlike, to make me into a deeper man, then I pray for . . . *superficiality!* I don't want to be deep that much. *Please* take away the pain." I wanted relief far more than I wanted depth.

But Jesus didn't take away the pain. And as I grew, I began to pray,

"Okay, Lord, then use this pain for your purposes. Use this pain to make me more compassionate. Use this pain to fuel my passion. Use this pain to take me to others in pain who need to know your hope in the face of suffering."

Passion is tough because it's usually connected to pain. But God calls us to imitate Christ—even to the point of allowing our pain to be used for his kingdom. Are we willing to say, "Lord Jesus, I invite you to use my dysfunctional past, my physical pain, my learning disabilities, my emotional pain, my brokenness—all to fuel passion for you and dedication to your mission in the world."

Exercise #4: Fire the passion to know Christ by fighting "passion-busters." We all confront things in life that squelch our passion to know Christ. When we identify these, we can determine to fight against them. I can think of at least three things that smother my passion. Maybe you relate to these, or maybe you have your own list.

Bitterness destroys my passion to know Jesus. Bitterness takes what could be powerful, positive emotional zeal toward Christ and detours it in a negative direction. When I focus on some unresolved hurt in my life—either toward God or another person—it distracts me from 100-percent focus on Jesus Christ.

The irony about bitterness is this: Although I direct my anger or emotion at someone who has hurt me, I'm the one who ends up getting hurt. Bitterness always exhausts and destroys the one who holds it—not the object of the bitterness.

Second, my desire for security waters down my passion. Our addiction to security, safety, and comfort—especially in the affluent world of the West—will almost always overtake the radical commitment that comes from passion. Passion involves risk. Passion involves abandonment of secondary purposes in favor of a supreme goal.

The story I told earlier—about leaving job security to concentrate more fully on reaching lost people—needs to be told with a footnote.

The conference that helped push me over the edge and make the decision to leave was part of a two-year process of gradually releasing my grip on my comfort-zone living. God had been telling me to move on and entrust my future totally to him, but my desire for security pushed down passion for God. I had a secure post, safe relationships, a steady salary—and I hesitated giving it all up.

Then I read a story in chapter 3 of Daniel. As the three young friends of Daniel face the fiery furnace of King Nebuchadnezzar, they refuse to bow down and worship him. So he stokes the fire even hotter—to the point that those doing the stoking drop dead. But as Daniel's friends face their own deaths because of their obedience to God, they tell the king, "The God we serve is able to save us from it" (verse 17). They articulate their faith, but then they state their passion to be God's men by completing the sentence with the condition *"But even if he does not . . .* O king, . . . we will not serve your gods or worship the image of gold you have set up" (verse 18, emphasis added). Their passion to obey God led them to the inevitable conclusion that security and safety is a secondary issue! When I read that story (that I'd read many times before), I made up my mind. I'll step out in faith and obey God—whatever it takes!

A *third passion-buster I see in myself is materialism.* As part of my affluent world of Western society, I can fall prey to the temptation to live for the pursuit of *stuff.* And when I do, my passion for Christ and his kingdom goes down the drain. Our societal desire for more and more, materially, douses the fire of passion. Our desire for increasingly more "things" means we spend our energies on earning and spending, accumulating and collecting. We fill our houses with more and more stuff, which then occupies more and more of our time—so that eventually we don't have either the energy or time for the passion of being 100-percent devoted toward knowing Christ Jesus.

SO, WHAT'S YOUR PASSION?

Dig into the core of anyone who demonstrates a sustained heart for people outside of Jesus Christ and we'll find a passion to know Jesus Christ. Everything gracious and loving that comes from us ultimately flows from our understanding of the gospel and what Jesus Christ has done for us. We'll see more of this in the next chapter. But here, let me restate the point, so that we don't overwhelm ourselves trying to reach out to our lost world:

A heart for lost people flows from our lives as we develop our passion to know Jesus Christ.

HEART BUILDER #1
GO CRAZY FOR GOD

I live in the American suburbs in a beautiful town. Many friends and neighbors hold college degrees, drive nice cars, and present themselves as dignified, respectable citizens. While I know that behind their doors there is relational abuse, alcoholism, and despair, people walk with heads high in my community.

How do I present the love of Christ in this context? I try to fit in. I act dignified, talk intelligently of my faith, and warm others to the gospel. If someone asks about our international missionary work, I talk about respectable things — like leadership development, well drilling in poor villages, and health care for children.

People listen and clap politely, but none get too excited about the Christ they see in me. They neither act nor react. What am I doing wrong?

When I looked more closely at the examples of Jesus and the apostle Paul as witnesses to God's truth, I discovered my problem—I'm simply not crazy enough.

Consider Jesus—he started his ministry, performed some healings, drew some followers, and then came home. And there, his family tried to restrain him because people were saying, "He is out of his mind" (Mark 3:21). The religious leaders called him demonized and his own household refused to believe (Mark 3:22,31-35; John 7:5).

Or look at Paul. He gets his big chance for ministerial influence in the political arena before King Agrippa, but rather than softly introducing the story of God's love, he gets right to the point—declaring the suffering Messiah whom God raised from the dead (see Acts 26:23). The listeners quickly observe that Paul, like his Master, Jesus, was out of his mind (see Acts 26:24). He had truly become a fool for Christ's sake.

When I first decided to follow Jesus, we lived in a countercultural era. We followers of Christ happily considered ourselves "Jesus Freaks." Being out of step with society was a good thing. We saw a little weirdness as evidence that our true citizenship was in heaven.

I wonder if I need to return to being radically different than the norm. Maybe my neighbors would rise up and take notice if I started welcoming the outcasts of the world into my dignified neighborhood. Maybe I should take my neighbors with me to the poorer world—so that they could see the countercultural nature of following Christ.

If I were a little wackier for Jesus, at least my neighbors would be forced to have an opinion—rather than relegate me into the category of a "nice, religious person." If being crazy for God was good enough for Jesus and the apostle Paul, it should be good enough for me.[6]

Some wish to live within the sound of church or chapel bell; I want to run a rescue shop within a yard of Hell. —C. T. Studd

HEART BUILDER #2:

REVIEW YOUR
BIBLICAL WORLDVIEW

God desires to bring people back
into a relationship with him.

While making my way through an international airport, I met a fellow pastor from a neighboring state. We hadn't seen each other for a long time, so we visited for a while. He enthusiastically told me about a conference from which he was returning.

"I think I've learned the *key* to mobilizing my congregation for outreach," he stated. "I just can't wait to go home and train them."

As I travel the country, I frequently meet other pastors and Christian leaders who are coming from or going to some conference. And often—like my friend—they go looking for the *key* to mobilizing others in outreach, evangelism, or even cross-cultural missions.

When Christian leaders desire to stimulate outreach, we often pursue a new training package, a novel technique that offers the "key" to effective outreach, or an instructional seminar. We think, "If people know *how* to reach out, they'll take action." We get home, do some training seminars, and give away the key, hoping our people will use it to unlock the door that keeps them from effective outreach.

But here's the problem. For many people, the question isn't "How?" The question is "Why?" Why reach out? Why open a conversation that will lead to difficult questions? Why become a bold witness and open myself up to the criticism of others?

The question is "Why?" because developing a heart for the lost speaks first to our motivation—not our method. What motivates me?

- To go beyond myself?
- To open my mouth about my faith at work?
- To start an evangelistic Bible study at my school or in my community?
- To reach beyond my comfort zone in the community and endanger my reputation for just being nice?
- To venture outside my church culture or network of friends to some lonely international student or first-generation immigrant?

Being motivated for outreach boils down to a matter of belief: "We believe, therefore we speak." So, before we look for the next instructional outreach video, we need to ask, "What do we really believe?" Our theological convictions about our faith fuel our passion for Christ (Heart Builder #1). We build our outreach on that foundation.

Our beliefs, however, stem from our worldview. Anthropologists explain that at our core is a basic view of reality—a worldview. That worldview determines who we are, what we value, and how we behave.

FOUR QUESTIONS THAT REFLECT OUR BIBLICAL WORLDVIEW

1. Who do we believe Jesus is? Christian outreach results from convictions about the servant example of Christ and his sacrificial death for our sins. If Jesus is just one of many religious options, motivation for outreach wanes. But if he is the only way, we find a compulsion to proclaim him to everyone.

2. Do we believe in eternity? Evangelistic zeal emerges from the mandate of showing lost people how to be saved through Jesus Christ. If we don't have a sense of heaven and hell, then we miss the eternal-life motivation for outreach. Urgency should flow from a sense of the realities of eternal fellowship with God versus eternal separation from God.

3. Does our Christian faith relate to the world? Is my faith a private matter, relating only to me and my world? Or does my faith address the issues of the times? If I don't believe that my faith is relevant, why speak up or venture into society? We'll look more closely at how we see ourselves as Christians in the world in the next chapter, but it emanates from a sense of what we really believe.

4. Does God want to use my life? Some people simply feel too small to make a difference. The vastness of human need can overwhelm us to the point of paralysis. We need to remember that God works mightily through the small, the insignificant, the mustard seeds to do his work in the world.

Maybe we don't need new evangelistic training options. Instead, we need to be clear on the foundational issues of belief that motivate outreach in the first place.

In Heart Builder #1, we looked at the example of the great first-century evangelist Paul to understand his priority of being passionate to know Christ. Let's look at Paul again—only this time focusing on his motivation for outreach to people outside of Christ. In Romans 1:14-15, Paul writes, "I am obligated both to Greeks and non-Greeks, both to the wise and the foolish. That is why I am so eager to preach the gospel also to you who are at Rome."

Although Paul's supreme desire was to know Jesus Christ, he lived as an overflow person. The fullness of his relationship with Jesus overflowed into a desire to tell others about Jesus. Like a young romantic, he just had to speak about the love relationship he had with Jesus.

TRANSFORMING HOPE

Paul completely believed in the ability of the Holy Spirit to transform people. Everything he did was built on the core conviction that we're in the business of being changed and being change agents—so that we all can grow into being "new creation[s]" (2 Corinthians 5:17) in Christ.

When Paul looked at people, he looked through the eyes of transforming hope. He believed that people could change, grow, and become spiritually reborn in Christ. He wrote, "God, whom I serve with my whole heart in preaching the gospel of his Son" (Romans 1:9), because he fervently believed in the power of the gospel to change lives! The vision of God's ability to change a person's life always motivates our wholehearted outreach.

I mentioned earlier that I became a Christian during a countercultural era—more precisely, it was in the days of the "Jesus Movement" (the late sixties and early seventies)—and so did my wife, Christine. This was a time of great spiritual awakening, and much of the excitement of this movement was built on the firm conviction that Jesus was powerfully able to change peoples' lives. Worship services seemed to regularly feature testimonies of some drug addict or derelict telling how he or she had been transformed by Jesus Christ. Many stories recounted miraculous withdrawal from heroin addiction. The stories exuded hope!

As a young Christian, I decided to go as a missionary to the University of Massachusetts-Amherst, a school that at the time had an incredible reputation for parties and wild behavior. Several Christian friends joined me, as we moved into the rowdiest dormitory on campus to bring the message of hope through Jesus Christ. We witnessed with little effect, but three years after college, a young man named Don— who'd heard our witness at school—wrote to tell me that his life had been transformed by Jesus Christ. More than twenty years later, Don is still faithfully following Christ. Thus, transforming hope through Jesus Christ shapes my worldview.

As a youth pastor, I struggled to reach out to churched kids who sat in the back rows, arms crossed, and obviously defiant against the faith of their parents. I remember Jim sitting there, critical and cynical because of all of the hypocrisy he saw in adults in the church.

But that's not the end of the story. In college, Jim entered into a life-transforming relationship with Jesus Christ. As he followed the guidance of God, he committed himself to global service, and now he's bringing the good news of the life-transforming power of Jesus Christ to people in Central Asia, through Bible translation with the Wycliffe Bible Translators.

The belief in the transforming hope of the gospel of Jesus Christ serves as a powerful motivator. Paul knew this as he wrote to the Romans. He believed in transformation because his own life had been transformed.

BACK TO ROMANS 1

Return to Romans 1:14 and following, and let's look at what theological truths established the foundation of Paul's worldview.

Paul wrote to the Romans (whom he'd never met) as he was on his way to visit them. He was writing about things that he wanted to discuss when he arrived. He was coming looking for "a harvest" (verse 13) of transformed lives.

The reference to "Greeks" (verse 14) raises the question, "Why does Paul speak of Greeks when he's writing to Romans?" The answer is that Alexander the Great's conquests had taken the Greek language and culture all over the world. A Greek, therefore, was not only a citizen of Greece, but also one who knew the culture and mind of Greece. The phrase "Greeks and non-Greeks" was a statement of whether or not they had received a Greek education.

The phrase "non-Greeks" (*barbaroi*) often appears translated as "barbarians." Those who spoke Greek considered other languages as inferior ("bar-bar" being their mimicking of an unintelligible language). Paul reminds the Roman readers that there is no room for the cultural or educational snobbiness that might include the sophisticated and exclude the less educated. The good news about Jesus is for everyone! William Barclay summarizes, "What Paul meant was that his message, his friendship, his obligation was to wise and simple, cultured and uncultured, lettered and unlettered. He had a message for the world, and it was his ambition some day to deliver that message in Rome too."[1]

WHAT ACTIVATED PAUL'S HEART FOR THE LOST?

When we examine the life and ministry of Paul, we find at least four things that motivated his worldview and resulted in his commitment to reach out.

First, Paul acted out of *responsive love.* His motivation grew out of gratitude for the awesome love of God through Christ. Before witnessing to others, he focused on his own gratitude for all that he had received in terms of forgiveness and new life. God's love had overwhelmed Paul: forgiveness, reconciliation with God, a new start, peace with God . . . all at the expense of Jesus Christ.

Later in Romans, he reminds his readers of this magnanimous love of God, who loved us so much that while we were still sinners, God unconditionally loved us and Christ died for us (see Romans 5:8).

For Paul—who grew up learning that he needed to please a punitive God who based acceptance on performance of the Law—a loving God was a dramatic revelation. It compelled him to talk about Jesus! And like a person in love, he was excited about declaring the gospel that had rescued him.

Second, Paul's motivation came from a sense of **obligation.** He saw himself as a debtor (see verse 14). This obligation sprang from a divine sense of appointment: he understood that being a follower of Christ carried with it the obligation to profess him as Lord (see Romans 10:9-10). He saw himself as "called to be an apostle and set apart for the gospel of God" (Romans 1:1). To the Corinthians, Paul wrote of his sense of compulsion, "Yet when I preach the gospel, I cannot boast, for I am compelled to preach. Woe to me if I do not preach the gospel! If I preach voluntarily, I have a reward; if not voluntarily, I am simply discharging the trust committed to me" (1 Corinthians 9:16-17).

Obligation isn't a cool thing in our times. No one likes the idea of being in debt to others. We have no-fault insurance and prenuptial marriage agreements because we don't want obligations.

But Paul saw no problem with this concept. He understood that his life had been redeemed and reclaimed by Jesus. He was a grateful debtor to Jesus, who had purchased his salvation with his own blood.

Third, Paul was motivated by *a sense of excitement,* or *eagerness* (see verse 15). The word *eager* (sometimes translated "ready") implies anticipation, enthusiasm, a zeal to see something happen. Paul is *ready,* expectant, and excited about proclaiming the gospel of Jesus Christ to anyone who will listen!

He's not referring to the hesitant patient's grimacing remark, "Okay, Doctor, I'm *ready* for the shot." Instead, he's referring to a sense of positive anticipation, like me when I say to my wife, "Okay, Christie, I'm *ready* for that kiss."

Paul is salivating at the thought of preaching the gospel in Rome. He's fired up. We might say that he's psyched. He's looking ahead to what God is going to do. This is why he'll go on to write, "I am not ashamed of the gospel, because it is the power of God for the salvation of everyone who believes" (Romans 1:16).

Paul eagerly desired to preach the gospel in Rome because he wanted to place himself where the transformational power of the gospel would be most prominent. Where sin and need are most overwhelming, God's gospel power is often most evident.

The famous missionary to China, India, and Africa, C. T. Studd, understood this when he wrote, "Some wish to live within the sound of church or chapel bell; I want to run a rescue shop within a yard of Hell."[2]

C. T. Studd perhaps inherited this eagerness to proclaim Christ from his father, a wealthy British socialite. When Studd's father was a new Christian, he asked the great evangelist D. L. Moody what social functions were permissible now that he had become a Christian.

Moody, himself an eager and excited evangelist, replied, "Mr. Studd, you have children and people you love; you are now a saved man yourself and you want to get them saved. God will give you some souls, and as soon as you have won a soul, you won't care about any of the other things."[3]

Moody was right. One of Studd's converts was his son, who later in life caught the same zeal. Young C. T. Studd wrote of the great exhilaration of seeing others come to know Jesus Christ:

> I cannot tell you what joy it gave me to bring the first soul to the Lord Jesus Christ. I have tasted almost all the pleasures that this world can give. I do not suppose there is one that I have not experienced, but I can tell you that those pleasures were as nothing compared to the joy that the saving of one soul gave me.[4]

Fourth, Paul was motivated to share the love of Jesus Christ because he believed in the **lostness of people without Christ.** He knew that without a Savior, people stand condemned before God.

In an age of pluralism, this is a tough statement. Most of us want to practice tolerance, an "every-person-to-his-or-her-own-way" philosophy.

But when Christians begin to accept this spirit of pluralism, we sacrifice the proclamation of the gospel, because pluralism would mean that people aren't lost. Paul believed the contrary.

> For all have sinned and fall short of the glory of God. (Romans 3:23)

> For the wages of sin is death, but the gift of God is eternal life in Christ Jesus our Lord. (Romans 6:23)

However, Paul wasn't glib about the lostness of people. His heart was broken about it; he wept for the separation between people and God. He wasn't pridefully thinking, "I've got the truth and you don't." Instead, he wanted to do everything in his power to see lost people come to Christ. Thoughts of lost people caused him "great sorrow and unceasing anguish" (Romans 9:2). He wrote of his own willingness to sacrifice his salvation so that others might be saved:

> I could wish that I myself were cursed and cut off from Christ for the sake of my brothers, those of my own race, the people of Israel. (Romans 9:3-4)

and

> Though I am free and belong to no man, I make myself a slave to everyone, to win as many as possible. (1 Corinthians 9:19)

If we love people, our hearts will break over their lostness and impending judgment. Compassion changes the way we look at our friends who don't trust Jesus Christ. Compassion changes the way we pray for the lost materialist, the renegade racist, the abortion-clinic doctor, and the promiscuous hetero- or homosexual.

Concluding that hell is a reality isn't a license to condemn, scorn, or forget those who are unsaved. Instead, the horrible reality of judgment fuels our compassion for lost people.

In the history of the advancement of Christianity, many great evangelists and missionaries caught Paul's vision of people condemned without Christ. Hudson Taylor, pioneer to the interior regions of China, wrote home to England to recruit others with images of the millions of lost souls in China cascading over the cliff into a Christless eternity. The young C. T. Studd left a lucrative career as a professional athlete (he was a champion in cricket) in England to go to China, India, and Africa. He wrote, "How could I spend the best years of my life in living for the honors of this world, when thousands of souls are perishing every day?"[5]

Several years ago, I had the awesome privilege of preaching the Easter services at our church. I knew that on Easter Sunday, I'd get to speak to more than a thousand people who come to church only once a year. I knew that many had no living, vital relationship with Christ, and I would have the opportunity to tell them how to come into such a relationship.

To prepare myself, I listened to one of my favorite sermons by a preacher named Louis Paul Lehman. The sermon, "Sinner's Day," outlines a sinner on trial before the holiness of God. After the sinner is condemned for violating every one of the Ten Commandments, he realizes that he has a hopeless case. In desperation, he calls for Jesus to save him, and the courtroom erupts with praise. Jesus presents the sinner before God the judge and says, "Father, this is one for whom I died. Do not hold his sins against him.[6]

I listened to that tape because it took me through the realities of sin and redemption all over again. It reminded me of God's great love, the work of Christ on my behalf, and my hopelessness without Christ. Remembering the gift of salvation made me eager to preach the gospel to others. I listened to that tape before preaching that Easter—so that

I'd be reminded of the theological foundations of the faith I was declaring to others.

Paul's zeal for evangelism and outreach grew out of a sense of gratitude, divine call, eagerness, and the realization of people's lostness without Christ. What motivates us?

- Maintaining our dignity to the point of never being embarrassed or rejected?
- Popularity, so that we never challenge people's views?
- Wanting to be "peace-at-any-price" people in relationships?

If our motivation is any of these, then we'll probably avoid the work of proclaiming Christ to others.

But if we desire to live out our convictions—as Paul did—that we should declare God's love, that we're called to be his witnesses, that we can eagerly anticipate a great harvest, and that people without Christ are lost, then *proclamation* will become our priority!

BIBLICAL PICTURE OF A HEART FOR THE LOST

Living out a biblical worldview means that our behaviors and relationships reflect the fact that God desires to bring people back into a right relationship with himself through Jesus Christ. Sometimes it helps clarify the implications of that by looking at characters in the Bible and how they expressed their own hearts for people who were outside of a relationship with God.

From the very beginning, when sin entered the world through Adam and Eve's choices, God has been initiating and pursuing lost sinners because he wants us back in a relationship with him. In Genesis 3:9, God articulated his passion to restore lost sinners by asking Adam, "Where are you?" Throughout the Scriptures, God has been bringing people back into relationship with himself. And what's his primary method? People reaching people. We're his method of communicating his love and redemption to a lost world.

Moses often expressed his heart for the unreconciled among his own people by interceding zealously for them before God. He never rejoiced when others were condemned for their sins. Instead, he went before God and begged for their forgiveness. Moses reminds us that we never have the right to write people off and judge them ourselves. God alone is the judge. We intercede before God so that others might find his mercy.

John White observes that Moses' heart for his own lost people demonstrates the "acid proof of the true intercessor" because Moses loved people so much that he was willing to stand before God on their behalf. He prayed, "And if not [that is, if you, God, will not forgive their sin], blot me, I pray thee, out of the book which Thou hast written."[7]

John Stott reflects the heart of Moses through his own brokenness and compassion about the realities of hell. He rebukes any lightheartedness about hell and writes, "I repudiate with all the vehemence of which I am capable the glibness, what almost appears to be glee, with which the Evangelicals speak about hell."[8]

God didn't give us the doctrines of judgment and hell so we can write people off and treat their eternal destiny lightly. If anything, it should bring us to tears at the reality of condemned people without a Savior.

The Old Testament account of a couple of *freed lepers* has often been used as an example of sharing our faith out of gratitude for what God has done for us. After God defeats a siege of a city, they discover that the enemy is gone and now there is food to share. After celebrating for themselves, they remember the people in the city. With a sense of generosity, they say, "We're not doing right. This is a day of good news and we are keeping it to ourselves" (2 Kings 7:9).

Their story rebukes our silence. We have the good news—greater than any discovery of a stash of food—yet many of us remain silent. C. T. Studd wrote about his own life when he kept the good news to himself: "Instead of going and telling others of the love of Christ, I was selfish and kept the knowledge to myself. The result was that gradually my love [for Christ] began to grow cold and the love of the world began to come in."[9]

The prophets take a serious view toward the proclamation of God's truth. *Jeremiah* reflects the same sense of obligation that Paul lived with: "But if I say, 'I will not mention him or speak any more in his name,' his word is in my heart like a fire, a fire shut up in my bones. I am weary of holding it in; indeed, I cannot" (Jeremiah 20:9).

Ezekiel—from a similar time period as Jeremiah—takes the intensity of obligation a step further. He combines the themes of both responsibility and judgment. Ezekiel adds the sobering warning that if we have God's words and warnings and fail to speak, we'll be held responsible: "Warn them . . . if they repent, so be it, but if not, at least you're not accountable" (Ezekiel 3:16-21; also 33:5-9, paraphrase).

Ezekiel's intensity mirrors the New Testament message communicated through the small and difficult-to-understand book of Jude. *Jude* commands first century Christians with this unusual phrase: "Be merciful to those who doubt; snatch others from the fire and save them; to others show mercy, mixed with fear" (verses 22-23). Mercy mixed with fear. Good news mixed with severe warning. Snatch people out of the fires of hell; sound the alarm!

In the New Testament, we have the example of *Jesus*, who freely declared his intentions to go to people who'd never received the love of God. The *apostles* went about their evangelistic ministry with a sense of urgency and abandon—not caring about their own safety because "we cannot help speaking about what we have seen and heard [Jesus]" (Acts 4:20). *Peter* urged his readers to reach out because God isn't "wanting anyone to perish, but everyone to come to repentance" (2 Peter 3:9). *John* exhorted the New Testament church in the first century to reflect the love of Christ to the world "because [God] first loved us" (1 John 4:19).

From Genesis to Revelation, the message of God to his people of faith rings out: You are my agents of redemption in the world!

TROUBLESOME QUESTIONS ABOUT ETERNAL JUDGMENT

Most of us accept Paul's first three motives for reaching out to people without question. But what about the fourth motive, lostness, and its corollary, eternal condemnation or judgment? Should our evangelism be motivated by a sense of people headed for the fires of hell? Should we warn people if they don't respond to the good news?

Consider these four commonly asked questions about hell and judgment as you explore your own answers and formulate your biblical worldview.

Question #1: Are lost people really lost? In our age of politically correct vocabulary, we don't hear many references to those who are spiritually or eternally lost. We refer to people who are "not quite as far along in their spiritual pilgrimages." But terms like *lost* and *sinner* sound too harsh or blunt.

But Jesus called people lost. He declared himself to be the only way of salvation (see John 14:6). The apostles preached that "no other name" was adequate for salvation (Acts 4:12). Paul wrote to Timothy that there was only "one mediator between God and men, the man Christ Jesus" (1 Timothy 2:5). In other words, no other go-between exists. There's no salvation outside of Jesus Christ. People without Jesus Christ live out of relationship with God. And they are *lost*.

The implications of this harsh reality are clear. If people are lost and I'm one of God's agents of reconciliation in a broken world, I must rekindle my heart for lost people.

Bill Hybels states the mandate of evangelism with the simple phrase, "Lost people matter to God."

Ajith Fernando points to the vision of lostness that motivated some of the great heroes of Christian history:

> The seventeenth century preacher Samuel Rutherford once told a person, "I would lay my dearest joys in the gap between you and eternal destruction." Hudson Taylor said, "I would have never thought of going to China had I not believed that the Chinese were lost and needed Christ." D. L. Moody told an audience in London, "If I believed there was no hell, I am sure I would be off tomorrow for my home in America." William Booth (founder of the Salvation Army) said he would wish that his Salvation Army workers might spend "one night in hell" in order to see the urgency of their evangelistic task.[10]

A vision of hell and seriousness about impending judgment obviously motivated some of the great leaders in recent church history, but what impact will it have on us?

Question #2: Are the lost really bound for hell—an eternal separation from God? I preached a sermon on hell a few years ago, but I struggled to know how to start it. I decided to ask the congregation a question.

"How many of you would like some good news, some *great news* today?"

People in our church don't commonly respond to the preacher, so I asked it again. Finally, a few responded affirmatively, so I proceeded, "Today I have some *good news!* Even *great* news! The good news is this: There is a hell. There's a fiery, coming judgment, when Jesus, the righteous Judge, will come to judge the living and the dead. People without Jesus Christ will suffer as a result of their unpaid-for sins. My news is this: Hell is a reality; coming judgment is a reality."

At this point in the sermon, a few snickered nervously, wondering where I was taking them. Some seemed a little confused. These statements hardly qualify as good news to most of us. So I continued, "So what's the *good news*? There is definitely a hell—*but we don't have to go there!* Our sins can be paid for so that we don't need to fear Judgment Day! In order for the gospel to be truly *good news,* bad news must also be a possibility. Otherwise, the good news is just news."

The good news of Jesus Christ means deliverance from hell, judgment, and the condemnation of our sinful selves before a holy God. Yes, eternal separation from God is a reality, but we have the opportunity to respond to God's love through Jesus Christ—and then give others that same opportunity—so that we can receive God's forgiveness, mercy, and eternal life!

Maybe you're thinking that these kinds of beliefs about hell are too strong. Aren't there other options? Well, let's quickly look at what other options might exist:

Option #1: Hell doesn't exist or—if it does—no one goes to hell because, in his mercy, God intervenes whether people believe in Jesus Christ or not. This position is known as Universalism or sometimes Christo-Universalism. It claims that the basis of salvation is Christ's work on the cross—regardless of our response.

This may be the most pleasant option, but it violates biblical teaching on hell's reality, as well as the choice God gives us. If God saves us against our wills, it contradicts the biblical understanding that we are created as free moral agents.

Option #2: Only the really bad people go to hell: Josef Stalin, Adolph Hitler, Timothy McVeigh. All of the nice people get into heaven. Of course, the problem with this view is, Who determines which of us is nice enough? If we return to God as the one who measures niceness, then we come face to face with God's standard of holiness. Then we echo the psalmist: "If you, O LORD, kept a record of sins, O Lord, who could stand?" (Psalm 130:3).

The nice-people theory sounds great, but it violates biblical teaching on God's holiness and justice—the fact that his holiness requires payment for sin.

Option #3: Only "active rejecters" of Jesus Christ go to hell; everyone else gets saved. This view again violates biblical teaching on God's holiness and justice. And it also calls into question almost all motivation for evangelism. After all, if some can be saved without the Savior, why not all? And if hell is only for active rejecters, why go and preach Jesus to someone who's never heard of him? If I go to those who are already bound for heaven, then preach Christ and they reject him, they've gone from being saved through passive ignorance to being lost by active rejection. Where's the good news in that?

Option #4: Only those who come into a relationship with God through Jesus Christ as their Savior get into heaven. All the rest go to hell. This is the view most consistent with all biblical teaching. People still have free wills; they choose. C. S. Lewis articulated this by describing the choice of our lives—whether or not we will bow to Jesus and say, "Thy will be done." If we don't make this choice, then—at the judgment seat of God—he states back to us, "You want to live independently of me? Then I grant you your wish—your will be done." And we live outside of God's presence for eternity—something the Bible calls hell.[11]

In this view, Jesus' death and resurrection satisfy God's holiness and justice. People receive God's love as expressed in Jesus' sacrificial, substitutionary death. And our salvation grows out of what Jesus has done for us. This truly is good news.

What option do you believe? Let God's Word—not wishful thinking—shape your worldview.

Question #3: Should we hear more about hell? While people seem to accept discussions of topics such as the spirit world and the reality of Satan and his angels, we seldom hear much about judgment, hell, eternal damnation, or the concept of everlasting suffering for those who haven't trusted Jesus.

Dr. Ajith Fernando of Sri Lanka, author of *Crucial Questions About Hell*, notes that Jesus spoke and taught more about hell than about heaven. He observes, "If one generation neglects the doctrine of hell, the next generation will reject it."[12]

Question #4: Why do we so seldom address the subject of hell? *Perhaps we no longer believe that it's real.* John Patten, when serving as the British Secretary of State for Education and Science, came under fire for arguing that "Crime is rising in Britain because the fear of hell is declining." He argued, "Britain needs a renewed sense of damnation and hope of redemption in order to return to civility," and insisted that moral behavior declines because there's no fear of getting caught by God the judge.[13]

The spirit of our age says, "Everyone's going to heaven," and that "People who don't know God or Jesus won't be judged." God's Word says that the righteous Judge will separate the sheep and the goats, and some will go to "eternal punishment, but the righteous to eternal life" (Matthew 25:46). In contrast to the naïve optimism about those who don't know God, Paul wrote in 2 Thessalonians 1:7-9:

> This will happen when the Lord Jesus is revealed from heaven in blazing fire with his powerful angels. He will punish those who do not know God and do not obey the gospel of our Lord Jesus. They will be punished with everlasting destruction and shut out from the presence of the Lord and from the majesty of his power.

Pluralism says, "All ways to God are equal." In contrast, the Bible affirms that Jesus Christ and his death on the cross is the only acceptable sacrifice to a holy God. Jesus is the ransom, the payment, and the satisfaction of God's judgment. Jesus is the lamb, the sacrifice provided by God, "who takes away the sin of the world!" (John 1:29).

Writing to the Thessalonians, Paul affirmed their choice to trust Jesus: "They tell how you turned to God from idols to serve the living and true God, and to wait for his Son from heaven, whom he raised from the dead—Jesus, who rescues us from the coming wrath" (1 Thessalonians 1:9-10). To the Romans he wrote, "Since we have now been justified by his blood, how much more shall we be saved from God's wrath through him!" (Romans 5:9).

Maybe we have no sense of judgment, blame, or accountability. A. W. Tozer observed, "The vague and tenuous hope that God is too kind to punish the ungodly has become a deadly opiate to the consciences of millions."[14] Ajith Fernando echoes Tozer: "When they come under conviction and think that they should take the costly step of repentance, something inside them says, 'Don't worry, it's not going to be that bad.'"[15]

We convince ourselves that God's mercy exists but that his judgment and holiness don't. This false assurance is the scariest belief of all because it leads to a false confidence that has eternal implications.

Someone might say, "God loves me." Well, according to God's Word, that is true: "God so loved the world that he gave his one and only Son, that whoever believes in him shall not perish but have eternal life" (John 3:16). But keep reading; God doesn't force his love—everyone has a choice to accept or reject the Savior. John 3:18 states, "Whoever believes in him is not condemned, but whoever does not believe stands condemned already because he has not believed in the name of God's one and only Son." John 3:36 also combines this good news/bad news: "Whoever believes in the Son has eternal life, but whoever rejects the Son will not see life, for God's wrath remains on him."

The spirit of our age says things like, "You're not to blame," "You're a victim," and "It's not your fault." We live in a time when no one wants to suffer the consequences of wrongdoing. We want to escape the consequences of the law through legal loopholes. We want to attribute our bad behavior to our dysfunctional families so we're not held responsible. We want God to be merciful to us, no matter how we respond to him. Norman Geisler writes, "In this pluralistic age, it seems too harsh a punishment just for believing the wrong thing."[16]

The overwhelming reality of judgment should motivate us to pursue outreach to those with no opportunity to respond to the love of God through Jesus Christ. Indeed, if we believe in hell, then we feel the greatest remorse when we hear of people who have no opportunity to hear the good news. Oswald J. Smith of Toronto's People's Church used to say "that no one should hear the Gospel twice before everyone had heard it once."[17] He was burdened for those who had never heard, reflecting Paul's desire to preach, "where Christ was not known" (Romans 15:20).

In spite of the wonderful advances of the gospel message around the world, missions experts still estimate that between two and three billion people have no opportunities to hear the gospel and respond.[18] The doctrine of hell ought to burden us deeply and mobilize the church to get the good news to these people.

Maybe we don't hear about hell because we've lost the sense of the majesty of God. We don't have the reverent awe and fear of God that the Scriptures advocate. To many, God is nothing more than a kindly grandfather who rocks us and tells us "everything's going to be all right." Or he's a heavenly Santa we make requests to.

A drunken man once sat in my church office after staggering into a service. I shared the love of Jesus with him. He obviously knew some Christian doctrine because he replied, "I don't want to go to heaven because hell is where the party is; all my friends will be there."

He's horribly wrong. The Bible says that damnation will be "weeping and gnashing of teeth" (mentioned six times by Jesus in Matthew and once in Luke). Those whose names are not written in the Book of Life will be thrown into the "lake of burning sulfur" where they will be "tormented day and night for ever and ever" (Revelation 20:10). That's no party!

THE WORLDVIEW CHALLENGE

Anxious to rekindle the flame of love for lost people? Then look at them with new eyes, a new biblical worldview. Like Paul's zeal to preach to the Romans, we have a lot to be grateful for—so we respond by declaring that love to others. We have a lot to be excited about—so we anticipate sharing Christ eagerly with others. But we also have a lot to be serious about, like hell and coming judgment—so we respond under obligation and with urgency.

Lost people matter to God. Does your worldview reflect that they matter to you?

HEART BUILDER #2
THE POLITICALLY INCORRECT JESUS

How do we refer to people who are outside of God's kingdom? I sort of like the terms seeker or preChristian. But I'm realizing that these terms are overly optimistic. I've talked with a lot of spiritually self-satisfied people who aren't seeking God at all. When asked, "Would you like a deeper relationship with God?" they reply, "No." When challenged to wrestle with the questions of death or their own mortality, they prefer to avoid such deep subjects. If these folks are searching for spiritual answers, they keep it hidden—at least from me.

Other people use terms like *unchurched*. This term refers to people who seldom, if ever, darken the doorway of a house of worship. If *seeker* is overly optimistic, I wonder if *unchurched* is overly pessimistic. It concentrates on what people are not. Even if we accept the term *unchurched*, I disagree with its focus. My goal isn't to get people into organized religion. Rather, I want to be a catalyst in their relationships with God through Jesus Christ. (After all, many "churched" people might be clueless about a *personal relationship* with God.)

How did Jesus refer to people outside God's kingdom? With no concern for being politically correct, Jesus called people "lost." He described the salvation process in Luke 15 as pursuing lost things—a sheep, a coin, a son. After seeking out Zacchaeus, Jesus defended his outreach to this embezzler by stating that he had come to "seek and to save what was *lost*" (Luke 19:10, emphasis added).

Why would Jesus use such a strong term—*lost?* Zacchaeus was far from down and out—like some drunk or derelict whose lostness everyone could see. He'd achieved wealth and success (albeit in a questionable profession), and had a home large enough to host a good party.

Perhaps Jesus called him lost because he saw a life dedicated to the wrong priorities. Maybe Jesus was commenting on his eternal state—teaching listeners that a rich man in this life who is poor in his relationship with God remains eternally lost to hell.

Or did Jesus call him lost as a reflection of the seeking heart of God—going after sinners with the invitational "Where are you?" (Genesis 3:9)? Or maybe Jesus called him lost to teach the disciples their responsibility to reach out to people like Zacchaeus.

We truly don't know why Jesus used these words. But the words remain in Scripture. Maybe we need to return to this politically incorrect language simply to drive home the intensity of this spiritual state—and to stimulate our evangelistic outreach. People outside of Christ aren't just potential seekers, nor are they the unchurched. They're lost.

If Christians wish us to believe in their redeemer,
why don't they look a little more redeemed? —Friedrich Nietzsche

HEART BUILDER #3:

REVISE YOUR
PERSONAL WORLDVIEW

Jesus sends us out as influencers.

I asked several dozen people at church how they interpreted Matthew 16:18: "Upon this rock I will build my church; and the gates of hell shall not prevail against it" (KJV).

The general reply was "I think it means that we will be safe from Satan's attack."

I explained that this was indeed the promise of 1 John 4:4: "the one who is in you is greater than the one who is in the world"—that God will protect us. Then I revealed that Matthew 16:18 isn't a defensive verse promising we will be safe from outside attack. Instead, it's an offensive verse promising that *the captives whom Satan holds in his kingdom will not be safe from* our *attack.* As God's people, we can boldly take the offensive, going into the world to snatch Satan's captives away from him. God calls us to engagement and to storming the gates of hell in Jesus' name.

The initial responses of these people reflect the most typical pattern of the Christian church. We've moved, in evangelist Sam

Shoemaker's words, from being "fishers of men" to being "keepers of the aquarium."[1] We shy away from engagement: We move out of the city, we abandon hope in public school systems, we start Christian organizations as alternatives to the secular world.

While these actions often start as tools to better equip the people of God, they often result in disengagement and a move toward privatized faith and irrelevant Christianity. Christian organizations, Christian schools and universities, and Christian home-schooling lose their focus if we forget the goal—to strengthen the saints so that we might be sent back out into the world as salt and light; or, as we'll see later in this chapter, as those who transmit the "aroma of Christ" to our world (2 Corinthians 2:15).

An examination of the Christian world might lead observers to conclude that the mission of the church is to make sure that Christians are happy and content—something called "insular" Christianity. We focus on our own spiritual health, our own fellowship, and our own doctrinal purity—often at the expense of interaction with the world.

How do we see ourselves as God's people in this world?

- Living in the church as a fortress, protected from the world? Or being trained for advancement against the forces of evil?
- In pursuit of sinners out of the love of Christ? Or avoiding the potential harmful effects of being too close to sinners?
- Penetrating the darkness? Or avoiding it?
- Proclaiming our faith publicly? Or guarding our faith in private?
- Addressing our faith to mainstream society? Or living in our comfortable Christian cul-de-sacs?

George Hunter calls the privatization of faith "*mad* Christianity" (emphasis added). He explains that a person is deemed mad or insane if the world existing in his or her head doesn't connect with the world of reality. He says that for many Christians, faith, God, Jesus, and the world of the miraculous exists only in their heads and fails to intersect with daily living. Faith is mad when it exists in my mind but doesn't touch the real world.[2]

On the other hand, engagement means studying the issues of our day and interacting. Engagement means involvement; we don't hide ourselves in the church or in our own safety zones. If we act as the people of God, we will infiltrate this world with his love and values. This means rubbing shoulders with secularists, humanists, pluralists, and just ordinary sinners like ourselves. Why? So that they might see Reality (another word for Truth) lived out in relevant ways through us.

One of the problems of engagement, of course, is lack of time. We often get so caught up in activities related to the church that we unintentionally marginalize ourselves from the world. Bob Lupton, a Christian worker in the city of Atlanta, refers to this as the problem of "unneighborly neighbors."

Do strong loyalties to church necessitate disengagement from those who live next door? If so, I have a misconception of the role of the Christian in this world. I have understood the historic mission of the Church to be a proactive force, armed with vulnerable love, infiltrating every strata of society, transforming fallen people and systems through the power of the Spirit. It is tempting to allow the local church body to become our enclave of like-minded friends that provides a protective haven from the daily bombardment of destructive values. Yet engagement—not withdrawal—has always been the operative word of the Church militant. And love of one's neighbor remains its fundamental tactic.[3]

Will we make the time for engagement? It's a crucial question.

READY FOR INFILTRATION?

Any discussion of our self-view as Christians will eventually turn up the word *witness*. As we contemplate engagement and influence in our world, we'll come to the question, "If we're God's people with our hearts on fire for Christ and his kingdom, what's our *witness* to the world?"

But at this question, we often grow fearful because we think to ourselves, *But I'm not a preacher* or *I'm no apologist* or *I don't want to stand on the corner and preach.*

Our stereotypes stem from the way we've come to use the word "witness." For most of us, it refers to our verbal witness—how we talk about the glorious message of Christ. Because we think witness equals speaking, we *go out witnessing* and take *witnessing classes* or we read books that describe how to be better at engaging people in conversations about Christ.

I'm in no way discounting the importance of our verbal witness for Jesus Christ. But I'd like to expand our concept of God's call on our lives to be his witnesses. I want to challenge us to consider the fact that God's Word calls Christians to be witnesses who proclaim the love of God in Christ to *all the senses.*

FIVE-SENSE EVANGELISM

What does this "sensory evangelism" look like? Witnessing to all the senses emulates the question WWJD—"What would Jesus do?"—with questions like:

1. How would Jesus *sound?*
2. How does Jesus *taste?*
3. What does Jesus *look like* to those outside the faith?
4. What is Jesus' *touch* in the world?
5. How would Jesus *smell?*

God calls us to be his witnesses to the reality of Jesus Christ in our lives as he affects each of our five senses.

THE SENSE OF HEARING

Let's start with hearing, the sense that most of us associate with witnessing. Romans 10:17 says, "Faith comes from hearing the message, and the message is heard through the word of Christ."

This is what we evangelicals are best at. We *proclaim*. Ajith Fernando, when preaching out of 2 Corinthians 5, urged our church members to *persuade* people with all the vigor and enthusiasm of advertisers. We want to *present* Christ in words that challenge people to respond. So we *preach*. We *broadcast*. We establish tape ministries. We use the media.

We get training on how to evangelize, how to answer tough questions, how to start evangelistic conversations, how to start evangelistic Bible studies—so that people can hear the good news. As part of the sense of hearing, we bring friends to *hear* the good news through evangelistic speakers and Easter services and Christmas pageants. The goal: When people hear, they might respond.

Proclaiming the gospel to the sense of hearing also leads churches to give to cross-cultural ministry, investing in things like:

- Church planting in France—so that people can be evangelized.
- Preacher-training ministries in India—so that more preachers can preach.
- Bible translation in Chad—so that people can hear the Word of God in their own language.

Of course, presenting the gospel so people can hear never gives us license to be rude. We should express our witness to the world in love, so that our words don't become just a "resounding gong or a clanging symbol" (1 Corinthians 13:1). We must speak the truth in love.

THE SENSE OF TASTE

Jesus encourages his followers, in their witness to the world, to appeal to the sense of taste: "You are the salt of the earth. But if the salt loses its saltiness, how can it be made salty again? It is no longer good for anything, except to be thrown out and trampled by men" (Matthew 5:13).

Jesus says that the disciple is *salt*. The salt analogy communicates at least two or three thoughts at once. Some observe that, in the culture of Jesus' days on earth, salt was a preservative. Therefore, God's people serve to retard evil and preserve good in the world. Others note that salt was used as an expression of purity—its glistening clarity made it attractive as an offering presented in worship. Therefore, Christians should be purifiers in a tainted and stained world. Both of these applications carry powerful challenges—to ward off evil and to purify.

But Jesus' *primary* meaning refers to salt as a *flavor enhancer*. Christians are meant to add flavor to life's dullness. In a world filled with monotony and boredom, the Christian community should live life in such a way that it appears (and is) tasty, livable, and desirable. We Christians—filled with the Holy Spirit and living out the character of Christ—add zest and vigor to life. Eugene Peterson captured this sense in Matthew 5:14 in *The Message:* "You're here to be salt-seasoning that brings out the God-flavors of this earth."

Somewhere along the way, we went the opposite direction and began advertising Christian faith as a way to become dull: "We *don't* do this and we *don't* do that!" That's why some people see Christian faith as something to be put off until later: "Let me live my exciting life now, and then—when I get old and dull—I'll trust Christ too." Oliver Wendell Holmes poignantly stated it this way: "I might have entered the ministry if certain clergymen I knew had not looked and acted so much like undertakers."[4]

We're supposed to be the flavor enhancers of life. By living out joyful lives built on a foundation of hope, we live to improve the quality of the lives of those around us.

So what do "salty" people look like?

- They look for ways to add value to their workplaces—maybe as simple as bringing in donuts on a dreary Monday morning.
- They look for ways to help someone else out of the loneliness of life— by visiting a nursing home or dropping over to see a lonely neighbor.
- They influence their communities with the zest for Christ by assisting in things like the Parent-Teacher Association, community groups, or local volunteer service.
- They're not afraid of going into environments of tastelessness, because Jesus in them is the salt. They add flavor, serving as moral disinfectants in society.

"Salty" Christians also seek to add flavor to the world beyond their immediate reach by helping others improve their quality of life by:

- Giving generously to victims of natural disasters—or getting involved directly in relief efforts.
- Helping people economically through training programs and things such as "micro-enterprise development"—helping the poor to break out of the cycle of poverty.
- Building houses through groups such as Habitat for Humanity.
- Donating clothes or food to ministries for the homeless.
- Inviting lonely people over for a meal.
- Hosting a neighborhood block party.

One question I try to ask myself every day is, "Jesus calls me to be 'salt' in society—how can I add zest and flavor and quality to the lives of the people I touch today?"

THE SENSE OF SIGHT

Jesus also says that we, as his witnesses, appeal to the sense of sight: "You are the light of the world. A city on a hill cannot be hidden.

Neither do people light a lamp and put it under a bowl. Instead they put it on its stand, and it gives light to everyone in the house. In the same way, let your light shine before men, that they may see your good deeds and praise your Father in heaven" (Matthew 5:14-16).

Jesus compares his disciples to *light*. Light brightens. Light guides us through the darkness. Light warns us of danger.

Serving as Jesus' light underscores our role in dispelling darkness. Into a world dark with sin, we come as lights—not hidden or covered for our own private use, but shining brightly and publicly like a city on a hill.

Listen again to how Eugene Peterson expresses this in *The Message:* "God is not a secret to be kept. We're going public with this, as public as a city on a hill. . . . Shine! Keep open house; be generous with your lives. By opening up to others, you'll prompt people to open up with God, this generous Father in heaven."

Something we often overlook about both salt and light: Jesus does *not* say, "You are the salt *of the church*" or "You are the light *of the church.*" We're called to be salt *of the earth* and light *of the world.* When Rebecca Manley Pippert wrote *Out of the Saltshaker,* she understood that if we stay in the church, we'd never fulfill our role as salt and light *in the world.*

This is why I get very nervous about our program-oriented, busy North American churches where we offer a thousand-and-one options for growth—most of which appeal to the person who's already a Christian. If all of our time is spent with our Christian peers, something is drastically wrong. We go to church each week to renew our saltiness and clean up our light—so that Jesus can send us back out into the world, refreshed and strengthened. As his salt and light in the world, Jesus calls us to go back out—to be flavor enhancers and darkness dispellers in the world.

Being light means that we let people see our faith. We don't hide it or exercise our faith only in the family of God. Instead, we speak up, act out, and go public with our faith. Being light is being, in the words of Oswald Chambers, "conspicuously Christian." There's no room for privatized faith!

And our light, Jesus says, is manifested by good deeds, kind actions, and demonstrated love. We don't do good deeds to be recognized or applauded—Jesus condemns that (in Matthew 6). Instead, we go about our lives of service and compassion and mercy ministries—and people will notice!

What do darkness dispellers look like?

- In the workplace, they tell clean jokes to overtake the off-color ones others tell.
- In the neighborhood or in the college dormitory, they host drug-free, immorality-free parties to show that you don't have to sin to have fun.
- They look for the darkest places and they move in—such as the staff of Youth with a Mission who moved into the prostitution district of Amsterdam, Holland, to plant a church between a house of prostitution and a church of Satan (see Floyd McClung's *Living on the Devil's Doorstep*).

Want your light for Christ to have the maximum effect? Find a dark place and penetrate that darkness.

THE SENSE OF TOUCH

To investigate the fourth sense that our witness in the world appeals to, consider Matthew 25:31-46.

Without stretching the text too much, I'd like to suggest that Jesus is affirming here that as his witnesses, we appeal to the sense of touch. We're called to bring the touch of God's love to a broken world. We become the hands of Christ's mercy to a hurting world and to hurting people.

In this passage, Jesus paints a picture of Judgment Day when the saved (the sheep) are separated from the unsaved (the goats). These verses make me very uncomfortable—because the sheep are *not* selected because they believed the right things or went to all of the appropriate Christian activities. The sheep are affirmed because of the way that their lives touched the needy around them:

■ They fed the *hungry* and gave drink to the *thirsty*.
■ They invited in the *stranger* and they clothed the *naked*.
■ They cared for the *sick* and they visited the *prisoner*.

Jesus emphasizes his main point twice, in effect saying, "By touching and serving these needy ones, you were touching me" (see verses 40 and 45).

"Touch" witness can take many shapes:

■ A Christian who works in the Finance District of Boston takes one lunch break every week and crosses a few blocks, where he serves meals at a soup kitchen for the homeless.
■ A woman who rides public transportation buys gift certificates from local restaurants so that she has something to give to those who beg.
■ A dentist dedicates a month each year to offer free services at a mission location in East Africa.
■ A couple goes through their clothes twice a year and gives what hasn't been worn to ministries that "clothe the naked."
■ A businessman starts a weekly outreach at a local prison.

Like Jesus' earthly ministry, our ministries—our witness to the world—must involve touch. And not just the touching of the beautiful people or the people who will thank us or the people who will help get us somewhere. Jesus' touch means touching the *helpless*, the *unclean*, the *social outcast*, and the *poor*. Think about that—is there any place in your life where you are giving without reciprocation?

The Sense of Smell

The final sense might be most surprising. As Christ's witnesses, we go into the world to appeal to people's sense of *smell*.

> But thanks be to God, who always leads us in triumphal procession in Christ and through us spreads everywhere the *fragrance* of the knowledge of him. For we are to God the *aroma* of Christ among those who are being saved and those who are perishing. To the one we are the *smell* of death; to the other, the *fragrance* of life. And who is equal to such a task? (2 Corinthians 2:14-16, emphasis added)

Paul tells the Corinthians that they are the fragrance — the aroma, the sweet scent — of Christ. He uses a vivid analogy that the Corinthians understood immediately, but we need some explanation.

He's describing a special parade by the Roman army called a "Triumph." A victorious general who had led an on-field conflict, killed at least five thousand of the enemy's troops, and extended the Roman Empire's territory would be honored with a victory march through the city of Rome to the capitol building. The march would proceed in this order:

1. State officials
2. Trumpeters
3. Those carrying the spoils of war
4. Others carrying symbols of the conquest — like models of citadels or ships that had been captured or destroyed
5. A white bull — to be sacrificed later
6. Captive princes, leaders, and generals chained together and headed for jail — or in many cases, to execution
7. Officers
8. Priests — carrying censers filled with burning incense
9. The victorious general in his glorious chariot
10. And finally, soldiers marching and shouting, "We have triumphed."

From that analogy, Paul says that we are the *aroma* of Christ. The risen Lord Jesus Christ is the *victor* and we go into the world as part of his "Triumph parade."

As his soldiers, we march through the world in triumphal procession because our Lord has won victory over death. So the fragrance of Christ is the *fragrance of victory*. But these verses also refer to the *fragrance of death*. What does that mean?

Consider that parade. If you were a returning soldier or a Roman citizen, the smell of the incense from the censers would mean victory. But for the captives, who smelled the same incense, it was the fragrance of death—it reminded them of their own imminent executions.

To the world, we are the fragrance of Christ. Our Christlike behavior, our attitudes, our work habits, our relationships, our service to others linger in the air—like a beautiful perfume or cologne. Did you ever enter a room several hours after someone wearing a strong perfume was there? It lingers. It creates a memory—even after the person is gone.

Unfortunately, our fragrance isn't always well received. To some we're the "fragrance of death" because our behavior makes them feel judged—even if we say nothing! After we declare our loyalty to Jesus, some people will apologize for swearing or cursing or anything else that they consider "unChristian." And they'll do this even if we don't say a word. Why? The presence of Christ in us carries with it both victory and condemnation. Light illuminates darkness and reveals that which was hidden. Salt stings as it heals. A touch can bring pain—even if it's part of the healing process. To some, we'll be the fragrance of death!

The idea of being Christ's fragrance is especially significant if you're seeking to be a witness to people you've worked with for years or family members who've heard the gospel message many times. In these situations, I enter by breathing the prayer, "Lord Jesus, guide my words and my behavior today so that something about my life leaves the fragrance of Christ. Help me to smell like Jesus today."

How do we embody the lingering fragrance of Christ?

- It could mean doing something anonymously in service to others — like raking neighbors' leaves or washing their car when they're not home.
- Practicing "random acts of kindness" to waiters, flight attendants, desk clerks, and service station employees.
- Guiding coworkers or peers in ethical and moral decisions — even without a biblical explanation.

Being the fragrance of Christ in the world means active service that leaves the scent of Christ's love lingering for others to ponder.

COMPLETE SENSORY EVANGELISM

We're Christ's witnesses. He sent the Holy Spirit to empower us. But we forget that our witness is a whole-life witness, to all of the senses: hearing, taste, sight, touch, and smell. The challenge is to grow to be complete witnesses. Ask yourself:

- To people's *hearing*, am I prepared to give a loving and well-thought *audible* explanation of the hope that I have in Christ?
- To people's *taste*, am I a "salty" Christian, a *flavor enhancer* who improves the quality of life of those around me?
- To people's *sight*, am I a light-of-the-world person who *dispels the darkness?* Am I conspicuously Christian? Do people see my good works and get pointed to Jesus?
- To people's sense of *touch*, am I the touch of Christ to needy people around me?
- To people's sense of *smell*, is there a *fragrance* of the love and life of Jesus Christ in my life that lingers — inviting people to think about eternal realities?

As you go into this week as a witness for Christ, review your life:

- How will I sound today?
- How will I add flavor today?
- How will I look today?
- Who can I touch today?
- How can I leave the aroma of Christ today?

HEART BUILDER #3
LOST PEOPLE—SEEN THROUGH TWO WINDOWS

To confront Christians in the Western world with global need, mission experts came up with the "10/40 window." This geographic block consists of all areas between the tenth and fortieth degrees of latitude, from West Africa to East Asia.[5] In this "window" lives 90 percent of the world's people who have never heard about Jesus Christ, close to 90 percent of the world's poorest of the poor, and a host of other superlative percentages, which should stir our urgency for prayer, evangelism, compassion, and missions.[6]

The people in our American pews, however, don't live in the 10/40 window. Most couldn't name any more than ten countries in this region. With the exception of news reports of breaking crises, most people aren't aware that this window—and its challenges—even exists. Addressing people's ignorance of the unreached constitutes a great challenge.

A second challenge emerges with local outreach. If we fail to look into the 10/40 window, can we at least look out our own windows? What about those in our own neighborhoods who don't know the love of Christ?

For our own neighbors, our busyness and preoccupation with Christian activities replaces ignorance as the obstacle to outreach. The opportunities for local outreach present similar invitations for prayer, evangelism, compassion, and missions. The magnitude may be less than the 10/40 window, but the immediacy is greater.

I spend much of my life mobilizing others for the 10/40 window. My travels have taken me to countries where Christians survive as a tiny percentage of the population, living under oppressive regimes. The needs of the 10/40 window inspire me to action.

But I live here. Out my window, I see the homes of people who never think about God, seldom attend any form of worship, and who suffer the consequences of a Christless life.

If I desire to be God's witness in the modern world, I need to learn to look *out* one window (my own) and look *into* another (the 10/40) so that I can respond appropriately with prayer, evangelism, compassion, and missions.

HEART BUILDER #4:

REBUKE
YOUR EXCUSES

———

Stop rationalizing.
It's time to look outward.

As a young Christian in a secular university, I joined a Christian fellowship that included a weekly commitment to go out and "do evangelism." We got together, prayed, broke into teams of two, and then went door to door in the dormitories or table to table in the cafeteria with a "spiritual survey" designed to engage people in conversations about their faith. We had many good and stimulating conversations, gave away a lot of literature, and amazingly had the privilege of leading a few people to faith in Christ.

I learned a great deal about sharing my faith over those weeks and months—about listening, about speaking in terms that people understand, and about responding to tough questions.

But I'm ashamed to admit one of the lessons I learned. Over those weeks and months, I became quite skillful at making excuses for not going out to do evangelism. My nonChristian roommate, Tom, brought me face to face with my ability to rationalize.

A group of us Christians were sitting in the lounge, preparing to go take surveys and invite people to listen to a gospel presentation by going through the "Four Spiritual Laws." We'd gone through training Tuesday night, which had closed with a motivational talk about evangelism from our campus leader. We went away excited that night.

But now it was Thursday night. The excitement had waned, and we weren't so sure of ourselves. We sat around the lounge, not knowing exactly where to start. I finally chimed in with some suggestions. I said, "Maybe tonight's a bad night to do this" (we were only a few weeks from midterm exams). A few agreed. I continued, "And maybe we should rehearse how to do the booklet with each other rather than insulting some nonbeliever with our shabby technique." A few more agreed, although someone pointed out that we had rehearsed our presentation twice on Tuesday night. Finally, I delivered the most spiritual perspective: "Well, I don't know about anyone else, but I think we should stay here tonight and commit ourselves to pray." Everyone nodded affirmatively; after all, who can argue with prayer?

That's when Tom, my nonChristian roommate, entered the conversation. He'd been listening from across the room. He walked into our group, grabbed a "Four Laws" booklet out of my hand, and said, "You know what your problem is? You're all scared and you're just making up reasons on why you can't do this. Give me the stupid booklet. I can read this to someone else."

We sat there in shock. Tom was right. We were afraid, and we were looking for excuses to keep us from leaving our comfort-zone spirituality. That night I learned that, like many Christians, I have the ability to rationalize when it comes to evangelism. We don't know what to say, so we hide behind spiritualized excuses. I think I'm more gifted in rationalization than I am in evangelization. The challenge that we face is to overcome our fears and rebuke our excuses.

THE FORGOTTEN FOUNDATION OF WITNESS

Maybe our tendency to rationalize comes from a wrong focus. We often turn to Acts 1:8 for the foundation of the challenge to express ourselves as witnesses of Christ's good news. In this pre-Ascension mandate, Jesus promises power from the Holy Spirit to be his witnesses in Jerusalem, Judea, Samaria, and even to the ends of the earth.

When we read the verse, we tend to focus on the command to "be my witnesses." For those of us interested in world missions, our challenge might focus on the concentric, ever-widening circles of outreach indicated by Jesus' geographical references. Or we might concentrate on the Greek word meaning "witness"—*marturia*—a powerful image-creating word of those first-century witnesses who were faithful to the death.

But our focus is still in the wrong place. The heart of the command "you will be my witnesses" is neither on us nor on the target areas. Instead, it should be on the power that Jesus will send from on high—the power of the Holy Spirit. For as he says: "You will receive power when the Holy Spirit comes on you."

For some Christians, the Holy Spirit is the unknown member of the Trinity. Still others only experience the Holy Spirit in the miraculous. But the Holy Spirit's work should be neither silent nor relegated to the exceptional and the miraculous.

The Holy Spirit carries out many roles in our lives. To name just a few, he sanctifies our character (see Galatians 5:22-23), teaches us in the truth (see John 14:16), and he gives us *power* to be witnesses.

In Greek, the word for power is *dunami*. We get the words dynamite, dynamo, and dynamic from this word. The Holy Spirit's power is explosive. But what does it mean to us in our daily discipleship of following Jesus? It means to us what it meant to those disciples to whom it was addressed in Acts 1.

Holy Spirit power means power over the fear of failure. It wasn't easy for Jesus' disciples to return to Jerusalem; they failed as witnesses there just weeks before. They ran from opposition. They denied Christ. They needed power to overcome the fear of the past failures that now dogged them. The Holy Spirit provides that power—for them and for us.

Holy Spirit power means power over feelings of inferiority. Jerusalem—the powerful urban center—was foreign territory to these Galilean fishermen. It was an intellectual and religious stronghold, and they were more like country hicks with distinguishable accents. So they needed power to believe that God could use their "blue-collar" message in a "white-collar" world. The Holy Spirit provides that power—for them and for us.

Holy Spirit power means power over ingrained racism. When Jesus identified "Samaria" as a locale for witness, the disciples probably shuddered a bit. Samaria was the home of the despised half-breeds who these Jews had been raised to hate. But Jesus said, "I'm giving you my Holy Spirit power so that you can overcome racism and see all people as people whom I love and died for." The Holy Spirit provides that power—for them and for us.

Holy Spirit power means power over fears of the unknown. Going to "the ends of the earth" sounds exotic to us, but to the disciples, the phrase would conjure up images of an unexplored world. They needed Holy Spirit power to launch them out of their comfort zones. The Holy Spirit provides that power—for them and for us.

Before we start addressing our specific fears and rationalizations, we must first acknowledge that this is the power we all need.

- Power to overcome our *feelings of failure,* so that we'll speak again as witnesses in our workplace and community, even if we've failed in the past

- Power to overcome *feelings of inferiority,* realizing that God can speak through us to the most powerful intellects of our day

- Power to overcome *ingrained racism,* so that the church represents the unity in diversity that God desires
- Power to overcome *fear of the unknown,* so we'll leave our comfortable places in order to tell another person about Jesus

COMMON EXCUSES

Even when empowered with the Holy Spirit, we still need to address our fears, our rationalizations, and our excuses.

"I won't know what to say." We express our heart for the lost in more than just words. Our witness is a whole-life witness (see Heart Builder #3 and the idea of "complete sensory evangelism").

Second, when we're speaking, we need to remember that we're partners with the Holy Spirit in evangelism. He can make our words adequate.

"My less-than-perfect life disqualifies me." Many of us have been plagued with the gnawing feeling of "I'm a lousy Christian; I'm afraid that my sins will discredit the gospel." While we do want to live lives of integrity before our nonChristian friends, we also need to remember that our message of salvation is all about God forgiving sinners. Some of my best witnessing moments have come after I've really blown my witness and called up my friends to apologize for my inconsistency.

When people say, "The church is full of hypocrites," I no longer object. I actually tend to agree—because I know I'm a hypocrite. I say one thing and do another. That's why I keep coming back to the grace of Jesus Christ for forgiveness. Keeping the perspective that I'm a forgiven sinner telling other sinners where they can receive forgiveness helps me realize that I'll never present a "perfect" witness—and I don't have to.

"If I say that Jesus is the 'one way,' people will think I'm pompous." In our pluralistic age, we think that talking about Jesus as "the way and the

truth and the life" (John 14:6) is a stumbling block. But we need to keep three things in mind. First, when presenting Jesus Christ, we're telling people what Jesus did, and we're inviting them to "taste and see" for themselves. People don't have to believe his uniqueness *before* they read the Gospels or see the life-changing power of Christ through people's testimonies. We can invite people to read the claims of Christ and decide for themselves.

Second, when we proclaim Christ, we can present the good news humbly—so that the accusation of being "pompous" goes away. We can listen to what others believe. We can act respectfully toward other faiths. In our age of disbelief in absolute truth, we might always be accused of being haughty—to think that we have the Truth and no one else does. But we don't have to inflame the accusations by being pushy or belligerent.

Third, we don't need to run from discussion about absolute truth and Jesus' uniqueness. If we entice people into the Christian faith by presenting it as "one among many options," but then claim that Jesus Christ is exclusive and that "no one comes to the Father except through [him]" (John 14:6), they'll feel betrayed and deceived.

"People really don't like talking about religion." One of the greatest challenges facing Christians in the "postChristian" world stems from the way that Jesus Christ, historical Christianity, and the contemporary church all get blended together. We need to remember that evangelism and outreach means presenting—by our words and deeds—the living Jesus Christ to people. We're simply inviting people to respond to the love of God expressed through Jesus.

Juan Carlos Ortiz challenges us to keep Christ as the focus of our witness when he writes,

All structures are a hindrance to people in their search for God. If people have to accept Christ plus the pipe organ, the piano, the program and the television ministry, millions will reject Christ. The more things we add to Christ, the more things people have to accept with Christ, the more difficult it is for them to respond.[1]

"People are too busy to think through these things." We live in a time when many people seem opposed to thinking about profound things like their relationship with God or eternal issues. Perhaps as salt, one of our roles in society is creating thirst for God. Our joy, our peace in the midst of conflict, our contentment may serve to make observers look at us and say, "I want what you've got."

But be patient. Live out your Christian life before people so that when they have a spiritual interest or a spiritual inquiry, you're there to offer a reason for "the hope that you have" (1 Peter 3:15).

PRACTICAL STEPS

When it comes to rebuking my excuses, regaining a focus on the Holy Spirit's power, and returning to the world as a witness for Christ, I've found three practical steps that serve as what I call "Fire Starters." They help consume my rationalizations and turn my attention to the "dynamite" power of the Holy Spirit.

Fire Starter #1: Reemphasize the gospel. I've gone to church for as long as I can remember. I came to a dramatic conversion at age seventeen, but even that was more than thirty years ago. I've observed a lot of sermons, meetings, praise songs, and Bible studies flowing under the bridge since then. I find that sometimes I grow complacent because I actually forget why I'm in the church in the first place.

Several years ago, during a particularly cool spell in my own spiritual life, I stumbled across an important lesson. Although I got "saved" back in 1971, I need to return to the basis for salvation daily. I need to celebrate what Jesus has done for me. Listening to a tape on Hosea by the great expository preacher Haddon Robinson brought me back to the basics. Like Hosea's prostituting wife, I found myself standing guilty before God. I found myself weeping as Robinson explained afresh the reality of the gospel, the depth of God's forgiveness, and the basis for my redemption through Jesus Christ. I found myself wanting to receive Jesus all over again.

Whenever I deal with my own spiritual apathy, I re-emphasize the gospel. I tell the story of God's work through the Cross, and it draws me back to Jesus with fresh and childlike wonder.

You might ask, "But how do we re-emphasize the gospel?" Here are a few ideas.

Preach it. "Easter," she said, "That's what got me started again." I had asked Nancy why she'd suddenly regained a new sense of excitement and energy about her faith. She explained that when she went to church on Easter, she heard the basic gospel. "The story of the crucifixion and resurrection reminded me of my Christian faith all over again," she said. "The reminder of the risen Christ revived me."

Easter presents only one opportunity. Whenever we can do our part to share the good news—leading group meetings, teaching Sunday school classes, or encouraging the pastor to give a basic gospel sermon regularly—we cultivate an ongoing spirit of revival for everyone.

Proclaim it. I never understood why Greg, an older, wiser Christian, used to start meetings at his home by asking people three questions, concluding with the question, "When in your life did you feel closest to God?"

He explained, "Many of the people we entertain are nominal or inactive Christians, but most at one time had made a personal commitment to Christ. When I ask, 'When in your life did you feel closest to God?' I'm trying to draw them back to remember that there once was a spark in their relationships with Christ."

Articulating where we came from in Christ can stir our own desire to rekindle our witness and our spiritual lives. The seemingly old-fashioned practice of giving our testimony provides us with opportunities to articulate the gospel—and it helps us realize what Christ has done for us personally.

Listen to the testimonies of others. The gospel gets re-emphasized when we're exposed to the transformational power of Christ. If we've become complacent, we need inspiration. Listening to people tell the stories of their own conversions through Jesus' love and power—or telling the stories of others through the use of biographies—can awaken us when we've fallen into the dozing spiritual state of "taking it all for granted."

Just listening to Ruth's story encourages my faith in God's transforming power. She writes,

My childhood was not a happy one for me. For you see, my dad was mentally ill. My sisters, my mother, and I were all abused physically and mentally. In fact, the abuse was so bad that I grew up believing my dad would one day kill our entire family. Needless to say, our address was well known to the police. I was very lonely and very depressed as a child. I didn't have many friends because my sisters and me were told to stay at home when not at school.

One bright spot in my childhood was that the school I attended required that everyone attend daily church. So I went to church for about eight years straight. I really didn't understand what was going on but I can tell you it was a very peaceful place for me. At church, and almost every night, I prayed that God would make my dad well. I really believed there was a God but that's about as far as it went.

As time went by I went away to college. The first two years I didn't attend any church. I still had many family problems and it was taking its toll on me. Then, I began to think about going back to church. I tried several in the area. Then I heard that there was a place that many students attended. It was called The Christian Center. After just one time attending I couldn't believe how different this place was. I came to find out that this church was different because it was filled with God's presence. I kept going back. I joined fellowship Bible study groups that were held on campus. I slowly came to understand who Jesus was. I became a believer and knew that Jesus died for me! I finally knew who God was!

I am thankful that God allowed me to be in a family that had a lot of problems. I now know that God allowed me to endure the many hurts so that I would seek him out. I now am certain that God blesses me and is with me during any trial that I face. I know I am not alone in this world.[2]

Ruth's testimony of redemption encourages my faith and boldness in witness. No people are outside the boundaries of his love—whether they come from an abusive home or have damaged their own lives.

Every year our church hosts a group of men from a Boston ministry that introduces people who are addicted to drugs or alcohol to Jesus Christ. These men lead our worship with fervent singing seasoned with dramatic stories of how God rescued them through the love of Christ. When these delivered drug addicts stand up and sing, "Jesus set me free," they inevitably motivate us all in our witness—because through them we review the life-changing power of Jesus Christ in our own lives.

Get alongside new Christians. Nate helped start our church more than fifty years ago. At age seventy-something, he still glows with an excitement and vitality in Christ. Such a saint provides an awesome model to imitate, so I asked him his secret.

"I teach a class of new believers and seekers, something I've been doing for thirty years," he replied. "If I have a secret, it's that I'm always articulating the gospel to new believers or inquirers."

"Do you do this for their sake?" I asked.

"No. I do it for mine; they keep me vital in my own walk with Christ."

Perhaps Nate illustrates one way to resuscitate ourselves from a state of spiritual apathy: get together with new believers. This will take us into contexts where we need to explain our faith, and we can relive the joy of watching others as they discover that *everything* is new.

In my travels to other churches, I've noticed that some of the most bored Christians pride themselves that they attend a Sunday school class that's been meeting since 1856. Maybe that's the problem—they have no exposure to new Christians. Elderly people who hang around with other elderly people tend to feel much older than do elderly people who hang around with babies. The same is true when it comes to our spiritual ages. New life gives life to everyone it touches.

Fire Starter #2: Take our eyes off of ourselves. Sometimes our spiritual apathy cloaks a deeper problem: We fall into boredom with our faith because we're too preoccupied with our own needs and problems. In short, we become full of ourselves and we begin to shrivel spiritually. Someone has said that the smallest package in the world is a person all wrapped up in himself! Our challenge? To look outward—to the needs of others.

Simple acts of service get us out of our complacency and into thinking about others. Taking the Sunday school class to a nursing home or to serve a meal at a soup kitchen might not give us opportunity to preach, but it certainly restores our sense of being the touch of Christ and the fragrance of Christ in the world. We come back revived because the biblical principle is clear—we find ourselves by losing ourselves (see Luke 9:24).

At our church, the unmarried young adults group presented a particular challenge with respect to their zeal for outreach. Sometimes they seemed to be self-absorbed. But their pastor, Dave, turned this group around. They began exploding with new life because they started emphasizing service to others. Nursing home visits, local outreaches to the community (they painted the town bandstand), ministry across cultures, and clothing donations for the poor all have served to strengthen the committed and revitalize the bored.

Teaching children gets people thinking outward. Bill, an executive in a local computer company, told me that his Christian faith had stagnated, "until I started teaching second grade."

Why? "It reacquainted me with the energizing stories of faith, and it forced me to explain the 'old, old story' to children who were hearing it for the first time. For the first time in years, I got excited again about reading my Bible, praying, and going to worship on Sunday morning."

Getting out of our comfort zone often ignites a spiritual fire. In our church, cross-cultural mission teams have revived the personal faith of many long-standing Christians. When we can get people into situations where they *must* trust God, their spiritual alertness intensifies. I've heard many stories about how people's spiritual lives were dry, but then they signed on to a mission team in hopes of helping others.

In one form or another, the follow-up reports have come back, "I went to help others, but God revived me—from trusting God for the finances, preparing for the ministry, and going through any number of 'if God doesn't get us through this we're not getting out' situations!"

Fire Starter #3: Come back again to the fullness of the Holy Spirit. In his book *How to Reach Secular People*, George Hunter III observes that even in the Christian church, "A vast number of people in western culture are no longer Christian disciples by anyone's serious definition."[3] His statement illustrates both a behavioral and informational problem in the church: People don't "act" Christian, and this often stems from the fact that they don't understand what being a Christian truly means. They remain uninformed.

In other words, our apathy might grow simply because we don't know where to find our source of joy. We understood what it meant to start as a Christian, but we never learned how to walk in faith day by day.

Go back to the basics: God wants us to be filled with the Holy Spirit (see Ephesians 5:18), live by the Spirit (see Galatians 5:16), and demonstrate the fruit of the Spirit (see Galatians 5:22-23). In short, he invites us to be filled with who he is daily so that eventually our character becomes like his.

Campus Crusade for Christ's *How to Be Filled with the Holy Spirit* and *How to Walk in the Spirit*[4] (or some other dynamic, equivalent resource) should be *must* reading for any of us desiring to stir ourselves out of complacency. Our zeal to see others revived means we need simple, articulate, and usable tools to help us explain to others the power for living that God makes available to us through the Holy Spirit.

The Holy Spirit is our source of power for true *life* in Christ; our witness starts in his power. Whether it's renewing our passion to know Christ, our compassion for lost people, or our dedication to be the salt/light/hands/smell of Christ in the world, the Holy Spirit is our source of power.

"Lord, revive me. Bring me back to spiritual vitality so that I'm witnessing out of a sense of an overflowing fullness of the Holy Spirit. Restore to me the joy of salvation."

HEART BUILDER #4
THE SCOPE OF OUR OUTREACH

Just what does it mean when we talk about "outreach"? Does it mean hosting a community-wide vacation Bible school? Does outreach include sponsoring of food drives to feed the poor? What about showing the *Jesus* film to our neighbors or coworkers?

Jesus outlined outreach in Acts 1:8: "But you will receive power when the Holy Spirit comes on you; and you will be my witnesses in Jerusalem, and in all Judea and Samaria, and to the ends of the earth."

■ Jesus first defines the fuel of outreach: Holy Spirit power.

■ Then he describes the essence of outreach: to be his witnesses.

■ Then he outlines the scope of our outreach: Jerusalem, Judea, and Samaria, and the "ends of the earth."

Outreach to Jerusalem constitutes Jesus' mandate for outreach right where we live—right where we're best known—even where we might have failed miserably in the past.

Oswald J. Smith, an advocate for global missions, knew that all outreach must start where we immediately find ourselves. He said, "The light that shines the furthest shines brightest close to home."[5] Outreach isn't some activity "over there." It starts where we live.

Outreach to Judea took the disciples to their wider region. For us, if Jerusalem represents our community, then Judea might be our county, state, or province. Judea outreach means cooperation for the impact of Christ's kingdom just beyond ourselves, beyond our normal spheres of influence.

Outreach to Samaria intensifies the challenge of true outreach because it takes us outside of our own ethnic people. To the disciples, Samaria was geographically close but culturally distant. They couldn't touch the Samaritans without intentionally leaving their own people. For us, Samaritan outreach takes us out of our comfort zone to serve those who live geographically close but whose cultures or living situations mean they're outside of our normal reach. This might include people who are ethnically different than us, people living in long-term care facilities, or prisoners. Bridging cultural, linguistic, and even historical barriers that separate us, Jesus commands us to reach out.

Outreach to the ends of the earth launched the disciples into the world. Jesus commands us to leave the familiar and follow the example of Old Testament Abraham—going out without knowing exactly where God would take us (see Genesis 12). The fourth circle in our rippling-out outreach takes us into global ministry—involving us in the work of Christ's kingdom around the world.

In the regions Jesus listed, only the first one could have had any tangible benefit to the disciples. The last three meant outreach elsewhere—for the benefit of someone else. Do our ministries conform to Jesus' scope of outreach—rippling out from our own communities to the world? Are we invested in outreach that might not immediately benefit our ministries and ourselves?

*Kindness has converted more sinners than zeal,
eloquence, or learning.* —Frederick W. Faber

RESEARCH
YOUR AUDIENCE

Understanding people increases
our effectiveness.

Over the course of several months, I developed a friendship with Bill, a local guy who I met at the gym. He knew I was "religious," but most of our conversations had been in the distant third person—talking about religious people in the news, the faith of the president, or Christian history.

We finally had time to sit down over lunch. I knew that Bill had some church experience behind him, but I assumed nothing—or so I thought. As our conversation progressed, I thought it was a good time to insert a blunt "gospel" question I'd learned in evangelism training. So I asked, "Bill, have you ever heard the message that God loves you and offers you the free gift of eternal life?"

"Yes," he said. "I've heard that many times, but can I ask you some questions?"

I nodded yes.

He went on, "My questions are these: What do you mean by 'god'?

What do you mean 'god loves me'? And what's 'eternal life'?"

My conversations with Bill over the years have pointed out to me my own need to understand the people I'm trying to reach. Heart Builder #2 addressed God's worldview concerning lost people. Heart Builder #3 addressed our worldview of ourselves—as God's influencers in the world. Now this Heart Builder addresses the spiritual worldviews of our nonChristian friends: How do they see the world? More importantly, what do they hear when we're trying to communicate the greatest truth in the world?

AMBASSADORS FOR CHRIST

Paul calls us "Christ's ambassadors" (2 Corinthians 5:20). This analogy underscores our need to understand where our listeners are coming from. Being an ambassador in the political arena usually means:

- Serving in a foreign land.
- An ability to communicate the message of our king or ruler to those in another kingdom.
- An ability to understand the culture of our recipients enough to make sure that we communicate our message accurately and clearly—in terms they understand.

We're ambassadors for God's kingdom in three similar ways:

We serve our King in a foreign land. Sometimes our own values seem opposed to the world's. That's why the New Testament writers refer to God's people as "aliens and strangers" (1 Peter 2:11). By coming into the kingdom of Christ, we often fall distinctively out of step with those outside of Christ. But this isn't a license to withdraw; instead, we're sent back into this foreign kingdom as ambassadors and "peacemakers" (Matthew 5:9) so that we can communicate our King's invitation to reconciliation.

We're sent to convey our King's message. As ambassadors, we're always looking for ways to communicate our King's message of love to those living outside his kingdom.

We work hard at understanding. Communication goes two ways. In order to increase our effectiveness as ambassadors, we want to understand the culture of our recipients enough to make sure that we communicate our message accurately and clearly—in terms they understand. This doesn't require an adversarial relationship with "the world." Tim Downs points out that understanding involves "finding common ground" where we can connect.[1] In the words of Steven Covey in the bestseller *Seven Habits of Highly Effective People,* we need first to understand before we worry about being understood.

To reach his audience, Jesus spoke in analogies they could understand—like farming and coins and family. To reach the audience at Pentecost, God enabled Peter and the apostles to speak in each listener's vernacular. To reach the people on Mars Hill, the apostle Paul quoted from their poets and drew on things he observed about their beliefs.

In the same way, we must always be on the lookout for ways to increase our understanding of the people we're trying to reach—with the goal of communicating the love of Christ to them in the most effective, understandable ways.

CHARACTERISTICS OF SECULAR PEOPLE

When we speak about Jesus, we often invite people to God's gift of eternal life. To the religious, such an invitation sounds appealing, but what about unchurched people? I confronted a secular perspective on eternal life as Kate shared her story.

> One of my greatest fears, probably since I was at least 8 years old, was the very promise God made through Jesus Christ—life everlasting.

The thought of living forever terrified me. I was unhappy with who I was. I was unhappy with life, and I hated the thought of being me forever. I did whatever I needed to do to bring me happiness, but I knew the things that I did were wrong, and they didn't work, they made me more unhappy with myself, so why would I want to live forever?[2]

If I approach someone like Kate offering the "good news" of eternal life, it comes across as "bad news." She operates from a fundamentally different worldview than I do. If I want to communicate Jesus Christ, I need to start by understanding Kate's view of the world and then respond to it.

George Hunter offers an excellent place to start—especially if we find ourselves steeped in "Christianized culture" and language. He helps us understand the worldview and belief systems of those living in our society.

Hunter lists ten characteristics of secular people.[3] Consider each one, and our challenge to respond.

Characteristic #1: Secular people are essentially ignorant of Christianity. As I've learned in my dialogues with the "Noon Platoon" (my local community swimming buddies—see appendix B), we Christians often speak a foreign language with our religious jargon, biblical analogies, and spiritual terminology. One fellow thought the Sermon on the Mount was when Jesus preached on horseback. A young Christian who'd come to faith out of a totally nonreligious background thought the Great Commission was 30 percent. And few people (even churched people) can quote the Ten Commandments.

Our challenge in responding: We certainly can't abandon biblical language. Rather, like missionary Bible translators, we must look for ways to communicate truth and ideas in terms and concepts that people understand. This might mean the use of images in the secular media or of terms we discover in our friendships and conversations with people.

We can always be on the lookout for "redemptive analogies" in culture, in language, and in nature — commonly understood illustrations of biblical truths.

Characteristic #2: Secular people are seeking *life* before *death*. Most secular people are looking for life *now*. They live as existentialists — as if this life is all there is. As a result, the "death orientation" of many evangelistic presentations (questions that start with phrases like "If you were to die today") may not be effective. Even secular people who *do* think about death don't necessarily fear eternity. They fear extinction — ceasing to be. They wonder about "when I am not" rather than "what will I do when I face God." Secularized people don't typically ask about life after death; instead, they want to know about life before death.

Our challenge in responding: Although we may be the catalysts that get people wrestling with the issues of life and death, our presentation of Christ's reality cannot be relegated exclusively to a "next-life" orientation. Our challenge is to live out and then proclaim the abundant, here-and-now life that Jesus promises.

Characteristic #3: Secular people are conscious of doubt more than guilt. In general, most people have little or no guilt about sin (either individual or corporate). We regularly hear in the news of criminals who commit violent actions yet express no remorse. Guilt has, according to Hunter, been replaced by skepticism, doubt, and even fear. Many people express this attitude toward God's good news: "It seems too good to be true — so it probably is."

Our challenge in responding: We need to be patient. Secular people don't simply dive into the optimism of Christian faith. They want to watch us and see if what we say we believe really works. They're doubtful of an orderly universe and a God who loves them, so the neat and tidy gospel we often present seems trite. We need to take the time to build relationships and say, in essence, "Watch the reality of Christ in me, and then make your decision." Michael Green states it this way: "Nobody will believe you have a new life unless they see a new lifestyle. And when they see it, they'll be ready to listen about the new life—and not before."[4]

Characteristic #4: Secular people have a negative image of the church. Hunter notes that secular people doubt the church's intelligence, relevance, and credibility. (I've watched enough questionable Christian TV broadcasts that I often doubt the church's intelligence, relevance, and credibility!) I once engaged in conversation with a fellow traveler named Isabelle, a French woman with a totally secular worldview. When she heard I was a Christian, she replied with total disbelief, "You're a Christian? But you seem so intelligent!" The irrelevance of the church often leads people to be indifferent: "It's okay for you, but it's just not what I'm into."

Our challenge in responding: When we speak of "the church," we can't do it passionless or critically, because we *are* the church. There is no Christianity for loners. Christianity is not just an individual following Jesus; it's also a follower of Jesus entering into relationship with other believers. But let's face it—one of the great struggles we face with being part of the church might be accepting who else is on our team.

So, the objective challenge involves working within our churches to make sure that our corporate faith is intelligent, relevant, and credible. And the subjective challenge means trying to respond to people's spiritual curiosity by presenting Jesus Christ rather than organized religion.

Characteristic #5: Secular people have multiple alienations. Alienation from nature, from any sense of belonging in community, and from untrustworthy political systems leaves people feeling isolated and alone.

Our challenge in responding: The story of most new Christians describes the process where someone befriended them and the long-term friendship eventually helped them open their hearts to Jesus

Christ. People need to see that we care, that we'll love them unconditionally, and that we'll be true friends—even if they don't respond to our evangelistic efforts.

Characteristic #6: Secular people are untrusting. Hunter says that people don't trust others, their leaders, or God. In marriage, they see betrayal as common. They've grown accustomed to leaders who lie to their faces; they don't even expect to be able to trust them. They see catastrophes and genocide and they conclude that either God doesn't care or that he's powerless to stop people like this.

Our challenge in responding: We need to be friends who can be trusted. Every story that I tell in this book has been cleared with the person it's about. Why? Because I don't want anyone to think I'm just using our relationship to illustrate my teaching. I want to be trusted. I want my word to be trusted. I want to repeat the experience of a few years ago when a nonChristian friend, after going through several great losses in life, simply said, "Thanks for being there for me." Building trust means focusing our friendships and really being there for others, because people will often trust that God cares for them and loves them because we've cared for them and loved them.

Characteristic #7: Secular people have low self-esteem. Loss of dignity and self-worth is a natural result of alienation, loneliness, and detached lives. To tell people "God loves them" might be inconceivable to the person who feels unloved or grew up in a context of abuse. Hunter makes the point that people don't differentiate between God and the church. If the church is judgmental—about divorce, sin, and lifestyle—then God must be too.

Our challenge in responding: Maybe we need to realize that "instant" evangelism is no longer possible (if it ever was). Developing a heart for lost people means entering their lives and getting involved—even in their messes. Again, people will believe that God loves them because we've loved them.

Characteristic #8: Secular people experience forces in history as "out of control." AIDS, global disasters, and the impersonal forces of the global economy lead people to conclude that "no one is in charge." This results in atheism (there is no God), agnosticism (if there is a God, he created the world but he's detached and uncaring about it now), or bleak pessimism (God doesn't like bad things to happen, but he's powerless to stop it).

Our challenge in responding: While we can't orchestrate this, our greatest witness to the world may be the way that we respond to crises, personal loss, or disaster. Christians involved in caring for AIDS patients or in rebuilding homes after an earthquake help communicate to the world that God is still in charge and that we don't need to succumb to hopelessness.

For Christie and me, in our own personal lives, our responses to health and personal crises seem to have been our greatest witness. We've tried to react to personal storms with a God-provided joy and peace that our nonChristian friends could observe.

Characteristic #9: Secular people experience forces in personality as "out of control." The breakdown of families combined with an increased awareness of our own personal psychological problems has created a "culture of victimization." "I'm not to blame" attributes our personality problems to our emotionally distant fathers and domineering mothers. We're more aware of dysfunctionality and emotional and physical abuse than any generation before us. The tendency to blame others for our shortcomings makes it difficult for us to communicate the concept of personal sin, accountability, and judgment. But the Bible is clear that all have sinned and each of us will give an account.

Our challenge in responding: Every person presenting Christ to another culture will eventually need to speak prophetically, but perhaps the best way to do this is through our own personal testimonies.

Through Christ, we can testify that we're not victims, that we're not defeated by the inadequacies of our parents, that we don't need to live lives of defeat because of our dysfunctional tendencies. We can tell our stories—and in them illustrate that God enables us to confront our own shortcomings and grow past them.

Characteristic #10: Secular people can't find "the door." Even those who search for God may despair that they can't find him.

Our challenge in responding: The gospel message builds on hope. We live as agents of hope in the world. We can help people find the door by sharing how Jesus Christ makes God real and allows us to have a relationship with him.

PRACTICAL APPLICATION: SEVEN WORLDVIEW QUESTIONS

E. Stanley Jones served many decades as a Methodist missionary to India. Many of his techniques and approaches changed the way Christian mission is done in India. Perhaps his most notable innovation was the "round-table" discussion. He'd invite leaders of various religions to sit at a table where he'd pose various questions, like "How does your religion address the issues of pain and suffering in the world?" or "Where do you believe that sin and hardship in the world came from?"

Jones believed in the supremacy of Jesus Christ, but he also believed that he needed to listen so that he could understand the best way to present the supreme Christ. He believed that missionaries to India had done too much preaching without enough listening. So he decided to listen to the worldview of the Hindu, the Moslem, the Sikh, the Jain, and the Buddhist—with the goal of understanding each worldview and then trying to address these worldviews with the reality of Jesus Christ.

Another missionary veteran to India, Lesslie Newbegin, wrote *Foolishness to the Greeks* to remind us that we—in the Western world—need to lay the same groundwork in our culture as people like E. Stanley

Jones did when they first went to India. We need to ask questions, listen, seek to understand the worldviews of others, and *then* respond with a relevant, understandable presentation of Jesus Christ.

In order to further understand the worldviews of people outside our Christian religious framework, consider seven questions we can ask — to help us *listen*. Evangelism specialist George Hunter observed, "Most effective evangelism does not involve *presenting*, in the sense of a one-way presentation of the Gospel, as much as two-way *conversation*"[5] (emphasis Hunter). I agree, and I offer these questions not as tools to help immediately launch into evangelistic presentations but rather to assist us in understanding and relationship building with those outside of the Christian faith.

Please note that these questions are a framework for designing your own questions. Most of my unchurched friends don't have a well-articulated philosophy of life, so asking them "What's the meaning of life?" (Question 1) may draw a blank stare or a sarcastic "To party every weekend." I doubt I'd ask that; so instead, I'd ask something like:

- "If someone asked, 'What are you living for?' what would you say?"
- "In the business world, everyone's talking about having a 'personal mission statement.' Do you have a personal mission statement?"

Realizing the need to personalize these, consider these seven questions:

Question #1: The meaning of life question. If we hope to communicate that Jesus provides meaning and purpose in life, we need to discover what people are already living for. This discovery comes by listening to their conversations, asking them to articulate their dreams, or going to their homes to see how they invest their money and time. For some Westerners, their clear life-purpose is acquisition. For others, having great families or offering their children wonderful futures dominates their worldview.

Worldviews help us see what people are living for. The fundamentalist Muslim believes that dying a martyr's death secures a place in heaven. The fictional materialist investor Gordon Gecko, in the movie *Wall Street*, articulated his worldview with the blunt remark: "Greed is good." Others fall anywhere in between.

What do your friends think is the meaning of life? Do they have articulated worldviews? What does this teach you about how they might be attracted to Jesus Christ?

The following are specific questions you can ask:

- Is this life all there is?
- Is there meaning to life?
- Is there a supreme being?
- Does he or she communicate with humankind? If so, how?

Many Westerners (even some who call themselves Christians) live with a worldview of materialism: matter is all that matters. In essence and practice, they're communicating their belief that this life is all there is.

Others adopt an absurdist, existentialist worldview. Life's a bad joke. There's no meaning or purpose. Live for today. We often see this worldview in contemporary humor that concentrates on sarcasm and cynicism.

Seeking pleasure also dominates Western worldviews. In the United States Virgin Islands, the caption on the license plates states, "American Paradise." If pleasure-seekers are looking for paradise, it's of the "this-world" variety, and tropical beaches, nightclubs, and the party scene fill the vision.

Before we present Jesus Christ and the life he offers, we need to understand what, if any, purpose already rules the lives and thoughts of our nonChristian friends.

Question #2: The "D" word question. "How do you (and your worldview) deal with death?" This probably isn't a good icebreaker question for starting a discussion about faith. Indeed, our unchurched friends may have no response. Hunter observed that people today concentrate on the issues of life here and now rather than life after death, so our outreach efforts probably should not focus exclusively on the "Do you know where you're going after you die?" question.

Yet, everyone deals with this reality at some point. Our finality causes us to search for meaning in our existences. Someone said, "Philosophy, after all, is ultimately the study of death." In other words, the reality of death forces us to investigate the meaning of life. Our search for purpose or our need for a worldview would be unnecessary if we knew that we'd live forever.

Death stands as a reality. We may run from it, deny it, or even avoid using the word, replacing *die* and *death* with "passed away," "departed," or "no longer with us." But the fact is that God has stamped an "expiration date" on our earthly containers, and we live (either knowingly or unknowingly) with that realization. That's why the writer of Ecclesiastes states that it's better to go to the "house of mourning" rather than the "house of feasting"—because "death is the destiny of every man; the living should take this to heart" (Ecclesiastes 7:2).

How do we discover what people believe about death and their eternal destinies? We can observe it by the way our culture deals with aging. Are we all trying to look younger and hide the decaying effects of aging? Ultimately, it signifies a fear of death. Do we avoid the realities of death—even to the point of making the deceased look better in their coffins than they might have looked when they were alive? It's probably because we're so "this-world" oriented.

Much of our proclamation of Jesus Christ comes as we address the issues of day-to-day life. But we can also apply a lesson from the church in Eastern Europe. When they were under the regime of Soviet Communism, pastors and church leaders often used funerals as their evangelistic outreaches. Why? Not because they were being insensitive to the bereaved, but because they knew that confrontation with death forced adherents of Communism to face a reality their philosophy and worldview did not address. And in the face of death, the pastors preached the hope that comes in Jesus Christ.

Over the past few years, I've had several opportunities to witness to the reality of Jesus Christ as the "resurrection and the life" at funerals. The grim reality of death has given an opportunity for me to discover that most of my unchurched friends live with worldviews that don't even raise the subject. Into that void, I've been able to articulate the hope we live with as Christians.

Question #3: The reality of suffering and evil question. I teach an undergraduate survey course on world religions, and in one of my first lectures, I state that all world religions fundamentally exist to address two questions: (1) What happens when I die? and (2) Why do suffering and evil exist in the world?

To understand where people are coming from, we need to talk about the problem of evil and suffering in the world. Rather than waiting for them to go on the offensive with questions like, "If your God is the God of love, why is there famine and war and cancer and AIDS?" I prefer to ask people first, "Why do you think there's so much misery in the world?" The question invites them to more thoughtfully articulate how their worldviews address the problem of evil, pain, and suffering. In most cases, people have no answer.

Worldviews differ widely in response to this question of suffering. The Buddhist says that our desire causes it, so the key to ending suffering is extinguishing all desire. The Christian Science adherent denies that suffering exists; it's all a figment of our imaginations. Those grabbing for the doctrine of "karma" in Hinduism, Buddhism, or New Age beliefs think that evil exists as the result of cause and effect — every bad action has a direct consequence. Of course, that doesn't explain why we may never know how one action connects to another consequence —

especially if we don't experience it until the next life!

I once participated in the funeral of a young woman, age thirty-seven, who died after a three-year bout with cancer. Her Christ-centered worldview let her live with an absolute assurance of God's presence. She exuded a sense of peace that Jesus was in control and that he would bring meaning out of her pain. At the funeral, I observed one of her coworkers, a devout follower of New Age Hinduism, listening to the Christian message. I found myself wondering how he evaluated all this? Was her pain just cruel fate, or suffering for her own sins in hopes of being reincarnated to try again? I prayed that God would use one of his purposes in her pain to introduce this man to Jesus.

When we raise the question of evil and suffering in the world, it forces us to ask what we ourselves believe. Volumes have been written on this subject, and this book is certainly not an apologetic concerning the problem of pain. But let me offer five possibilities in terms of God's role in this suffering world. I use these when talking through this particular worldview question with people. I review them and then ask, "Where do your views fall?" This may seem overly simplistic. But it helps people look at their personal beliefs and their perspectives toward pain, suffering, and evil.

Option #1: God doesn't exist. We're at the mercy of the impersonal forces of nature, fate, or some other unknown. Suffering exists because nature weeds out the weak through survival of the fittest. The theological framework of this view is atheism. If carried to its logical conclusion, it results in a worldview of despair—at least in response to human suffering.

Option #2: God exists, but he doesn't care. He "wound up" the world like an old alarm clock, and now he lets it go on its own. This worldview comes from the theological framework known as agnosticism. God is, but we can't know him. And he chooses not to be involved in the human condition. Agnosticism's response to human suffering and evil eventually comes to hopelessness; God leaves us to our own devices and offers no hope of rescue.

Option #3: God exists, but he's powerless to stop bad things from happening. This worldview builds off a theological framework known as dualism—where good and evil forces are equally powerful and at war with each other. Some Christians even espouse this worldview by attributing all personal suffering or natural disasters to Satan and his evil forces—with the implication that God is powerless to stop the crisis. A dualistic worldview may give us emotional or even sympathetic attachment to God, but it leaves us without expectation that he will intervene or the assurance that he will triumph over evil.

Option #4: God exists, but he's capricious. The belief that God is random and unpredictable can lead to the total submission in worship that we see in the most devout Muslims. However, this leaves little room for a two-way relationship based on love. If God acts one way in one circumstance and totally opposite in another, we can never be sure where we stand in our relationship or what he'll do next. The response eventually becomes one of fear. It can lead to extreme devotion—thinking that we'd better get on God's good side because we never know what he'll do next.

Option #5: God allows pain and redeems it. In this view, God allows evil and uses it. Some pain comes without apparent cause—cancer, a car wreck, famine. It simply reflects that we live in a sinful world. Other pain comes as the consequence of human choice—both personally and collectively (in other words, we suffer because of the evil choices of others, not just ourselves). But God's mercy intervenes, and he can even use pain and suffering for redemptive purposes. The greatest example of this is the offer of salvation achieved by the death of Jesus Christ on the cross. The worldview that results builds on hope. We hate pain and suffering, but know that pain can take on meaning.

Telling my nonChristian friends that I believe that "God is in control" no matter what can come across as trite to them—like a stoic or pessimistic acceptance of whatever happens. So I go on to explain that my trust in God's control means I believe:

- That he's working all things in human history toward his *ultimate* purposes.
- That nothing happens without his permission.
- That my personal pain can be used by God for purposes I may not understand or like.
- That bad things still happen because we live in a *fallen* world, living out the consequences of the accumulated bad choices of humanity starting with Adam and Eve. Bad things happen because of the introduction of sin into the world. This in turn breaks relationships—with God, with each other, and even with creation.
- That he still calls me to get involved in battling evil, alleviating suffering, and relieving those who are in need.

I also go on to explain to people what it does *not* mean when I say, "God is in control":

- It does not mean that I'll understand everything about suffering.
- It does not mean that God will fax me with a written explanation of all of his actions.
- It does not mean that I always think that God is fair (and I further explain that I've come to understand that his definition of *fairness* is often more long-term than mine).
- It does not mean that painful circumstances will make me happy.

Dealing honestly with the issue of pain and suffering can build a wonderful bridge to people who are wondering if God really cares.

Question #4: The personal evil question. Getting people to discuss the reality of evil *in the world* may be relatively easy. But how does their worldview deal with the problem of evil *in our hearts*? My question may start negatively: "How do you deal with your own propensity toward evil or wrongdoing?" Some will deny this tendency, but many honestly admit to their personal shortcomings—although they always qualify it with "But I'm not as bad as [some notorious tyrant]."

The first question then leads to the positive solution to personal evil. I'll ask, "Does your worldview include a solution to broken relationships through forgiveness? If you fail, how do you make a fresh start?" In other words, does redemption exist in your personal philosophies of life? What gives a person the ability to recover, rebound, and get back up?

The question sometimes leads to a discussion of solving problems of racism through reconciliation. Or it leads to people talking about people in the past they simply can't forgive. But the question helps me to understand whether or not my friends are looking for the release, fresh start, and new life that comes with Jesus' invitation of forgiveness.

Question #5: The truth question. How does your worldview approach truth? Do you think there are absolutes or is everything relative? How does your worldview address other worldviews? Do "all rivers lead to the same ocean" or do you think one belief is true and contrary beliefs are false?

In this age of pluralism, we might be able to predict people's responses. Everyone is okay—no matter what he believes. Asking the question allows us a window into a person's convictions about truth—so that we can understand the challenge it may be for him to read Jesus' words about being *the* way, *the* truth, and *the* life.

Question #6: The impact question. To find out where people stand in their personal sense of involvement in the world, I might ask, "What do you see as your responsibility to help 'fix' some of the world's woes?" Basically, I'm asking, "What impact do the followers of your worldview have on the world?" but in more personal terms. Is your worldview self-serving or other-serving?

This question stirred some great conversation at a seminar I attended. About twenty-five of us from the American Management Association were meeting in a nice training facility in New York City. The subject: Preparing People for Overseas Assignments. At the time, I served as the missions pastor of our church, and about 25 percent of my job involved training new missionaries.

The "What impact?" question came up as we discussed what motivated people to work overseas, especially in economically, socially, or politically challenging places. Nearly everyone else in the group pointed to one drive: profit. One person said, "If we don't offer a 30-percent increase in salary as an incentive, no one will even consider an overseas assignment."

I laughed and the attention turned to me. I said, "Sorry for laughing, but most of the people I'm recruiting take a 30-percent lifestyle *decrease* in order to accept an overseas assignment. The people I'm working with all go with a sense of a 'higher' call."

The only person at the seminar who understood the concept of "going for a cause" was the personnel director of the World Wildlife Fund, whose workers sacrificially dedicate themselves to saving environments and species nearing extinction. Everyone else was forced to confront a materialistic worldview that saw overseas opportunities only in terms of personal gain. My answers led to several conversations over meals; people wanted to know what motivated such sacrifice. I had the chance to share the challenge of following Jesus as a servant in the world.

Question #7: The relevancy question. What difference does a worldview make in daily living? Does it apply to daily chores, relationships, problems, and needs? Or is it removed from reality—advocating a detachment from the mundaneness of today?

When I asked this question of an associate, he testified glowingly of the impact yoga made in helping him deal with the pressures of daily living by helping him put problems out of his mind. Yet, as he explained his newfound ability to rise above the tensions of daily living, he discovered for himself that he had found relief by escapism, not by forging a relevant life philosophy.

When we ask the question of relevancy, we need to be sure that we have a solid answer. The old critique of Christians being "so heavenly minded that they were no earthly good" developed when we presented a gospel message that implied that only the "next life" or the "spiritual realm" was worth pursuing. If we're inquiring about the relevancy of someone else's worldview for daily living, we'd better make sure we've wrestled with the issue ourselves.

UNDERSTAND FIRST

These seven questions and their derivatives can help us understand where people live and what they really believe. As we listen, we can then look for opportunities to present our perspectives as followers of Jesus Christ.

When we start to evaluate all of the worldviews out there, we'll find that some of the stock solutions stacked on philosophical shelves aren't adequate to answer the greatest hungers of the human heart. We need answers that will satisfy our hearts, minds, and spirits. Jesus Christ provides that answer, but we need to understand the worldviews of others so that we communicate the answer clearly.

HEART BUILDER #5
BUILDING BRIDGES, BREAKING WALLS

The changing face of our world requires that we learn the skills of cross-cultural outreach. We need to learn how to communicate love, friendship, and the gospel to people from other cultures, languages, and nations—sometimes without even leaving home.

The concept of cross-cultural outreach comes up in other barriers between people as well: economic issues—poverty or wealth—separate people every bit as much as race or ethnicity. India may have an official "caste" system, but our culture divides easily along financial lines.

So what's the role of the follower of Jesus Christ involved in outreach?

Two analogies suffice: bridge building and wall breaking.

Bridge building means seeing people who are separated and seeking to bring them together. God exemplified this in that "while we were still sinners, Christ died for us" (Romans 5:8). We were separated from him, and he built the bridge through Jesus Christ.

Bridge building means the development of long-term relationships, coming into each other's worlds, and sharing in meeting needs. By doing this, we communicate the desire to build a bridge between the cultural, linguistic, ethnic, or economic gulfs that separate us.

Wall breaking, on the other hand, has a more forceful tone to it. It identifies the barriers between people and knocks them down. Paul writes concerning the divide between Jews and Gentiles that Jesus himself "is our peace, who has made the two one and has destroyed the barrier, the dividing wall of hostility" (Ephesians 2:14).

Through Jesus, we also aspire to break down walls that divide people. We serve as peacemakers, not just peacekeepers. Our outreach includes knocking down walls of injustice and breaking down issues (like language, humor, and other behaviors) that build walls between people.

Outreach means destroying walls and constructing bridges to communicate the love of God through Jesus Christ.

The problem today is that the spiritual situation is desperate, but many of God's people are not. —Vance Havner

REFRESH YOURSELF
WITH LIKE-MINDED PEOPLE

When we join with others who are
looking outward, it fuels our zeal.

Whenever I sense that my heart for lost people is waning, I do a little self-evaluation. Am I growing in my focused passion to know Christ (Heart Builder #1)? Do I look at lost people as precious individuals God desires to redeem (Heart Builder #2)? Do I see my life as a witness to all the senses of lost people around me (Heart Builder #3)? Have I rebuked my propensity to rationalize (Heart Builder #4) and dedicated myself to understanding the people I'm trying to reach (Heart Builder #5)?

If my self-evaluation sheds no light on my waning zeal, then I know—*it's time to get together with Richard Rhodes!*

Richard and I have been friends for more than a dozen years. Richard loves Jesus and he loves people—especially those outside of Christian faith. I get together with Richard just to listen. He always has a new outreach idea, and a new testimony of someone whose life has been transformed by Jesus Christ. He'll give me an update on his relationship with his Jewish-Universalist neighbors—who recently asked

Richard and Dori (Richard's wife) to study the Bible with them! He'll tell me about the work of others in outreach—because Richard trains others in evangelism. And he'll remind me that he prays regularly for my friends in the Noon Platoon—the friends I mentioned whom I swim with three or four times per week. When my "fire" for lost people grows dim, Richard frequently serves as God's agent to me—to fan my flame or restoke my fire.

A heart for the lost is not just about personal spirituality and worldviews. It's not about having all the right answers and techniques. It's about heart. Zeal. Enthusiasm to see the life-changing power of Jesus Christ at work in someone else's life. And if we intend to keep our heart for lost people strong, we need the help of like-minded people.

Where do we find these people? Most of us look immediately for people who are gifted as evangelists. But others can be equally stimulating. Look for a new Christian, whose zeal about being forgiven bubbles over. Look for people who have been dramatically saved—individuals who, like the apostles in the book of Acts, "cannot help speaking about what we have seen and heard" (Acts 4:20).

LIVING IN TWO WORLDS

As followers of Jesus Christ, we make up the people of God, the Christian community, and the church. But Jesus calls us to be *in the world.* He says, "As the Father has sent me, I am sending you" (John 20:21). And he prays for his disciples and us—not that God will take us out of the world, but that God will protect us from the evil one (see John 17:15).

Therefore, we live in two worlds—the *community of faith,* and the *community of the world,* where we live as tangible illustrations of the love of God through Jesus Christ.

As citizens of two communities, Christians can drift in two divergent directions. We can become extremists, either in our desire to influence the world or in our dedication to the Christian community.

At this point, you might think that I advocate the first extreme: abandon the church and go into the world. While I do vividly see the danger of Christians becoming insulated in irrelevant Christian community that withdraws from the world, I also know that the opposite extreme is equally wrong.

Derek's story reminds me of the need for balance. In reaction to what he saw as self-serving Christian communities, Derek decided that he didn't need Christian fellowship. He wanted to spend all of his time reaching out and influencing those outside of Christian faith. But Derek became isolated. He grew lonely.

His radical dedication to lost people didn't transform people or society as quickly as he hoped, and he got discouraged. Eventually his desire to be identified with people outside the church caused him to alter his lifestyle so that he fit in with his peers. He departed into what might simply be summarized as worldliness.

Derek's extreme reaction caused him to lose his spiritual edge, and he became indistinguishable from the very people he was trying to reach.

The opposite extreme—dedication to the Christian community and its corresponding escape from the world and secular society—creates an equal imbalance. As we'll see in Heart Builder #7, this extreme can lead to a different type of isolation and irrelevancy. We become salt in a community that's already seasoned. We keep our lights in a brightly-lit room rather than penetrating the darkness.

A woman at church told me, "I cry every time I hear the Lord's name taken in vain." I appreciated her sensitive spirit, but I wondered if she even knew anyone outside of the church world. With extreme devotion to keeping the Christian fellowship unstained from the world, we remove ourselves and begin to focus on who we're *not* rather than who we are as Christ's change-agents in society. We lose our mission. We become complacent, self-centered, and lukewarm.

At its worst, this extreme degenerates into infighting and judgmental attitudes toward each other. This hurts the community inwardly by creating divisions. And it discredits the community outwardly, presenting to the world our inability to get along together—the direct opposite to John 13:34-35, which describes a community of people who attract the world to Jesus because of their love for each other.

In contrast to either extreme, Jesus exhorts us to be a loving community permeating the world with our influence. We need balance. We need both the Christian community (this chapter), and to be out in the world (next chapter).

WHY WE NEED EACH OTHER

Why do I need time with my friend Richard to fuel my zeal for outreach in the world? Why do we need to come together with fellow Christians?

The Bible teaches that we need each other for a host of reasons. We have varied gifts. Together, we make up the whole that is the body of Christ. Our corporate worship brings us together before God in a way that individual worship can't. All these reasons mandate our participation in the Christian community. But consider five specific reasons why we need each other—as they apply to strengthening our heart for lost people and our broken world.

1. We need each other's encouragement. Hebrews 3:13 reminds us to "encourage one another daily . . . so that none of you may be hardened by sin's deceitfulness." Derek tried to live without Christian encouragement and he fell into a sinful lifestyle. He hardened himself against the convicting power of the Holy Spirit by rationalizing, "I need to reach these people, so I must become like them." He needed Christian friends to come alongside him and encourage him to identify with lost people without adopting their lifestyles.

Sin can harden our hearts in the opposite direction. We can become so tired or grieved at the effects of sin in our world that we want to withdraw into holy seclusion. We no longer want to touch the unclean world, so we withdraw. However, we need fellow Christians to encourage us to keep our hearts soft to those outside the faith—seeing them compassionately as Jesus did, "like sheep without a shepherd" (Matthew 9:36).

Mark, a local pastor in my area, dedicated himself to creating an atmosphere of encouragement in his church. He wanted to see people strengthened in their worship, but he also wanted to help them stay soft to the world they were sent into every week. He actively encouraged his church members to evangelize unchurched people. Mark says,

> I told them, "Jesus went to the parties of 'sinners'; therefore, we should choose to cut back on church activities so that we can go into the world of those outside the Gospel." They listened but didn't take me seriously until I missed a church reception (another nice gathering of those already in the Kingdom) to go to a party with some couples my wife and I were trying to reach."[1]

Without Mark's example, many of his church members would have been content just to stay with their Christian friends.

2. We grow stronger through corporate prayer. We need each other in fellowship so that we can go to God together in prayer. In prayer together, we can identify the challenges and opposition we might face as witnesses in the world and bring it all to God.

The early church as recorded in the book of Acts provides an inspirational model of the balance between prayer and outreach—going to God, followed by going into the world. By the fourth chapter of Acts, the religious establishment of the day wanted to put a stop to the preaching of Christ. They called in the apostolic leadership and threatened them, commanding them to cease with their evangelization and good works in Jesus' name (see Acts 4:5-22).

Peter and John went back to the Christian fellowship and reported the threats—and the anticipated punishment—from the religious leaders, and then they "raised their voices together" (Acts 4:24). They recalled the sovereignty of God, the prophecies of Scripture, and the sufferings of Jesus. Finally, they made their request to God. Instead of asking for deliverance from the threats, they asked, "Now, Lord, consider their threats and enable your servants to speak your word with great boldness" (Acts 4:29). Finally, they asked for the Holy Spirit's power to be evident (see Acts 4:30).

And God answered them. "After they prayed, the place where they were meeting was shaken. And they were all filled with the Holy Spirit and spoke the word of God boldly" (Acts 4:31).

Their prayer unified their dependence on the Lord and on each other and they went out as bold witnesses. Their community encountered the power of God (see Acts 5:1-11), and their witness in Jerusalem expanded. When physical beatings and persecution resulted, they found themselves "rejoicing because they had been counted worthy of suffering disgrace for the Name" (Acts 5:41).

Corporate prayer leads to corporate boldness. Turning our attention upward reminds us of who is in charge in the world—our sovereign Creator God. It reminds us of how he brings forth his purposes, even through hardship. And it puts us in the position of intentional dependence on the power of the Holy Spirit.

On several occasions, I've had the privilege of being in prayer meetings with George Verwer, the founder of Operation Mobilization, a global ministry with more than two thousand staff members. When we pray, George remembers the works of God in the Scriptures. He recounts the miracles of God in recent mission history. And then George presents his petitions—boldness for witness in the Muslim world, courage in the face of opposition in China, willingness to die if necessary, so that Jesus Christ might be proclaimed to all the nations.

These prayers renew my understanding of the phrase about the place being shaken. We're not afraid anymore. We're fired up and ready to go—across the street or across the Great Wall of China. Corporate prayer builds us up and gives us cooperative courage in the God who sends us out.

3. *Corporate worship and growth together assure us that we are not alone.* We need the fellowship of other Christians because the needs and challenges of the world simply overwhelm us. We need to know that we're part of a bigger team, God's team.

The writer of Ecclesiastes understood this when he wrote that "two are better than one" (Ecclesiastes 4:9) because when one falls, the other will lift him up. Our camaraderie in the body of Christ helps keep us from stumbling. We grow stronger because we discover that we're not alone.

Consider the disciples in the days preceding and following Christ's death and resurrection. In the last days of his life and following his death, when they got scared, they ran and scattered. They abandoned Jesus and each other. After the resurrection and ascension of Christ, they were still scared, but they stayed together and they prayed. And God came in power. The church came into being out of a corporate time of prayer and worship.

Worship precedes witness and worship provokes witness. Worship precedes witness because our testimony to the world overflows from our relationship to Christ. And worship provokes witness because when we're together, we realize that we have glorious good news to share with all people. From our worship we must go out to tell others about the God who loves us so much.

4. *We need others to recharge our spiritual batteries.* Living as God's people in the world puts us into spiritual battle "against the rulers, against the authorities, against the powers of this dark world and against the spiritual forces of evil in the heavenly realms" (Ephesians 6:12).

It's exhausting to live as light pushing back darkness. Proclaiming truth against falsehood wears us down. It's easy to get tired being the salt of the earth or the fragrance of Christ. We come together to find strength in our fellowship, our prayer, our study of Scripture, and our corporate experience of the person of Jesus Christ.

Why do you think Christians in persecuted countries risk their lives in order to meet and worship together? Why did Paul and Silas decide that their prison cell could be transformed into a worship center? Why do we need our regular times of gathering?

The answer to all these questions is the same: God made us to need fellowship. In our community gatherings, he recharges our spiritual batteries. Our growth together empowers us to go out again into the world.

5. *Our corporate fellowship cleans us up to send us out again.* Neither my wife nor I smoke, but several of our friends do. When we meet with them or drive them in our cars, the smell lingers. On one occasion, I came into the house after some meetings and Christie immediately asked, "Who've you been with today? You smell like you've smoked two packs of cigarettes!"

When we spend time in the world, it inevitably gets on us—like the lingering smell of cigarette smoke. If I avoid Christian fellowship for long stretches and associate only with my nonChristian friends, I find it easier to use profane language or I start thinking about off-color jokes I've heard, or I fall prey to coveting after the material possessions that they covet. I become like the people I'm hanging around.

If I'm in the world (as I'm supposed to be as Jesus' disciple), I get the world on me. That's why I need to come regularly to the gathering of fellow Christians. Christian fellowship is where I confess my sins and re-align my purposes with the purposes of God.

A ROMANTIC VIEW OF THE CHURCH

At this point, you might pessimistically assert that my view of the church is exceedingly romantic. If you're saying, "My church fellowship doesn't look like this," you're probably right. Many churches feature bored believers going through the motions of religious ritual. Only a few encourage passionate prayer for a lost world, and some Christians find themselves in Christian communities where they get criticized for going into the world as salt and light.

Why do Christians get bored, apathetic, or lukewarm concerning their own potential for outreach? Why do churches and Christian fellowship groups often fall far short of their mission to encourage and equip Christians to *go* into the world? Both the Scriptures and experience reveal that Christians can fall into a state of malaise or boredom for any number of reasons.

Churchgoers may not be believers. When Ruth, who equated churchgoing with salvation, joked with her brother Ed about his spiritual apathy in his young adult years, he snapped quickly back, "That was because I wasn't even saved yet!" Ed made his point: His apparent boredom as a Christian wasn't apathy; he was lifeless! Until his conversion, church fell into the category of family responsibilities instead of a personal relationship with the living God.

People sometimes might go through the motions of faith because of their parents' faith. Others hold to a misguided belief that going to church results in being a Christian. Some even have a commitment to knowledge and doctrinal purity without a life-changing relationship with Jesus. But all may give the appearance of spiritual apathy.

These folks don't need to be "re-vived" out of their boredom; they need to be "vived" because they've yet to meet Jesus, who alone can give them spiritual life.

The cares and worries of the world render the church fruitless. In the parable of the soils, the seed planted in "thorny soil" grew up alongside thorns, and these thorns choked the plant, "making it unfruitful" (Mark 4:19).

The cares and worries of the world choked the plant, but apparently without killing it. The plant still gives the appearance of being a plant; it's simply fruitless. For some, the unwillingness to separate from worldly priorities chokes out their spiritual lives. They show up at meetings and may even support the ministry financially, but their lives demonstrate coolness toward their faith—and especially to sharing their faith. They may give the appearance of being spiritually mature people, but their lives remain fruitless.

Individuals or the group preaches a lifestyle of self-reliance. Self-reliance epitomizes the teaching of popular religion and the psychology of our times: "You have the power within you"; "Think positive thoughts"; "Be your own boss."

Self-reliance kills spiritual vitality in two contrasting ways. First, overdependence on self leads to death by pride. This killed the vibrancy of the faith of the apathetic Laodiceans rebuked in Revelation 3. They thought of themselves as those who "do not need a thing." But God shined the spotlight on their need, highlighting that they were "wretched, pitiful, poor, blind and naked" (verse 17). Their only option? Repent of their self-reliance!

Second, overdependence on self can also lead to an opposite death: death by discouragement. Those expecting to "psyche" themselves into deeper spirituality often lose interest in the faith and give up. Thinking they just don't have what it takes to live as disciples of Christ, they quit trying. Simply put: many Christians limp along because they try to live the Christian life on their own power!

People are disappointed with the church. The church of Jesus Christ assembles together many not-yet fully sanctified people, and we hurt each other. Some refuse to forgive and move forward in relationships. They may boast of personal faithfulness to Christ, but their spiritual lives are listless because of preoccupation with all of the ways that others in the church have caused pain, been letdowns, or generally failed to live up to full Christlikeness.

In some cases, hurt-by-the-church people withdraw totally from the fellowship. Fortunately, their apathy doesn't infect others, and they simply need to be loved and discipled back into community. In the worst cases, however, hurt people stay in the church and contribute negative energy through a critical spirit or an attitude of bitterness. (See Hebrews 12:14-15 for the corporate destructive power of bitterness.)

People fail to tap in to the power of the Holy Spirit. Great theologians debate whether someone can accept Jesus as *Savior* without receiving him as *Lord.* But one thing is clear: We can't experience his transforming power and joy for life without being filled with the Holy Spirit and under the control of Jesus as our Lord every day (see Ephesians 5:18-20). This sets the foundation to walking in the Spirit and demonstrating the fruit of the Spirit (see Galatians 5). From the Spirit-filled life, our zeal for witness overflows.

HELP YOUR FELLOWSHIP REACH ITS FULL POTENTIAL

If our fellowship groups, Christian communities, or churches fall short of these ideals, then let's make it our priority to be change-agents from within. How?

■ Find at least one other like-minded person who can fan your flame for reaching lost people. A friend like Richard Rhodes can give you a real boost. If you can't find an encourager like this in person, get tapes from evangelistically oriented ministries or read the biographies of people who gave themselves to reaching out.

■ Work within your church to be an encouragement to others—challenging, encouraging, and exemplifying a lifestyle that reaches out beyond the church doors.

■ Infiltrate the prayer ministry of the church by turning the prayer requests upward (toward the sovereign God) and outward (toward our broken world).

■ Start a prayer meeting regularly with the one or two other like-minded people you do find—just to remind yourselves that you're not alone.

■ If your spiritual batteries aren't charged at church, find tapes or literature that encourages your own growth—and then go back into church with the intention of helping charge others.

■ Let your pastor and other church leaders know about your ventures into the world and remind them of your need to be cleaned up and sent out again every week.

HEART BUILDER #6
WHAT KIND OF BLESSING?

We all want God to bless us. Even if we have a tough time defining the term *blessing,* we know it's something good. Look at prayer-request lists or sit in on a small group's prayer time and you'll read or hear about prayers for blessing—from the economic: "Help Jim find a job"; to relational: "Guide Mike and Beth as they consider marriage"; to physical: "Please heal Joanne's cancer."

I wish we heard more prayers for effective outreach. But we don't. The objective listener might think that Christians go to God as some sort of cosmic Santa, sit on his lap, make our requests, and really hope that he'll come through for us.

Praying for God's blessing is perfectly biblical—provided that we maintain the bigger picture. Consider Psalm 67: "May God be gracious to us and bless us and make his face shine upon us" (verse 1). This prayer sounds like a plea for personal blessing, but the psalmist has something bigger in mind. His prayer is that God will bless *so that*:

- "[His] ways may be known on earth, [his] salvation among all nations" (verse 2).
- The peoples (of earth) might praise him (see verses 3 and 5).
- The nations might "be glad and sing for joy" (verse 4).
- God's blessing—symbolized to the psalmist as an abundant harvest (see verse 6)— will have the result that "all the ends of the earth will fear him" (verse 7).

What's the point? When we pray for God's blessing, we need to pray with a much bigger perspective—God's! Let our prayers echo the psalmist as we invite God's blessing *so that* others—especially those outside of God's family— might be blessed. Psalm 67 prayers might sound like this:

"Help Jim find a job, Lord, so that his witness might expand and his generosity increase."

"Guide Mike and Beth as they consider marriage; make their relationship a testimony of your grace to people who don't know you."

"Please heal Joanne's cancer so that she demonstrates your healing power; in the meantime, please bless others as she exhibits your peace in this storm."

God wants us to ask for his blessing, provided that we understand that he blesses us *so that* we in turn can be his blessing to the world around us.

HP (high potency in our relationship with Christ) +
CP (close proximity with those we want to influence) +
CC (clear communication) = MI (maximum impact)

—Bill Hybels and Mark Mittelburg

REENTER THE
WORLD YOU'RE TRYING TO REACH

The essence of Christian witness is
going into the world of another.

Several years ago, I attended a seminar in our area coordinated by The Navigators. Jerry White, Navigators' president, led the seminar. The workshop addressed the apparent inability of the Christian church to reach out to the secular world.

Whenever I attend a seminar like this, I want to come away with at least one memorable fact or challenging idea. This seminar began at 9:00 A.M., and by 9:15 I had my greatest challenge of the day. White was summarizing some research his organization had done concerning Christians and our intersection with the nonChristian world. As I recall it, he said: "Our studies reveal that after someone has come to faith in the Lord Jesus Christ, it takes just two years before almost all of their friends are Christians. To be specific, we found that the average Christian who has been a Christian two years has less than one nonChristian friend."[1]

I remember thinking, *fewer than one nonChristian friend!* I first found myself critical of the church that distracts people from going into the world, but then I looked at my own calendar. I read over my own prayer list. I thought through my own list of social contacts. *I realized to my own shame that—other than family members—I had no friends outside of my Christian faith.* My social life was filled with Christian encounters. I was on a church staff at the time, and my day was filled with contacts with Christians. I was a lousy neighbor; I'd never even seen some of my near neighbors, much less met and befriended them.

I determined that something in my life priorities needed to change.

CHANGING OUR FOCUS

Earlier, we looked at the biblical worldview, which sends us into the world, touching others through our "sensory" witness—to the hearing, taste, sight, feel, and smell. The concept is that we're "out there"—living and interacting with the people we're seeking to reach. We've used words like *engage* and *influence* and *touch.*

We minimize our influence, however, if we insist on remaining in the safety of our Christian subculture. Mack Stiles writes, "This is a dangerous temptation. Many Christians don't know a single non-Christian on a social basis and associate nonbelievers only with images on TV or statistics in newspapers. We forget that they are flesh-and-blood people with real hurts, dreams, struggles, and loves."[2]

Simply put, we demonstrate our heart for the lost by our propensity to be with them. Do I have any nonChristian friends? Do I pray daily for anyone outside of the faith?

Howard Snyder calls outwardly focused people "kingdom people"—in contrast to "church people." He writes, "Church people think about how to get people into the church; kingdom people think about how to get the church into the world. Church people worry that the world might change the church; kingdom people work to see the church change the world.[3]

Evangelist Sam Shoemaker points out that the focus of the church has changed:

> In the Great Commission the Lord has called us to be, like Peter, fishers of men. We've turned the commission around so that as stated earlier we have become merely keepers of the aquarium. Occasionally, I take some fish out of your fishbowl and put them into mine, and you do the same with my bowl. But we're all tending the same fish.[4]

In the excellent book *Becoming a Contagious Christian*, Bill Hybels and Mark Mittelburg build their book from this formula:

- ■ HP (High potency in our relationship with Christ. For our purposes, this parallels Heart Builder #1—passion to know Christ.)
- ■ + CP (Close proximity with those we want to influence. That's the topic of this chapter.)
- ■ + CC (Clear communication—see Heart Builder #5, "Research Your Audience.")
- ■ = MI (Maximum impact.)[5]

If we want to build a heart for the lost, we need to build friendships, reach out, and go into their world. Like missionaries going into a foreign land, we need to enter the culture we're trying to reach if we're going to address people with the gospel in terms that speak to their needs—in words that they understand.

HOW **NOT** TO DO IT

Henry Drummond reminds us that sometimes those of us who call ourselves Christians distract nonChristians from hearing the message of

God's love: "How many prodigals are kept out of the kingdom of God by the unlovely characters of those who profess to be inside?"[6]

Why do we fail in our efforts to reenter the world we're called to reach? Author Dick Staub identifies three negative postures of Christians in the world.[7]

Posture #1: Cocooning. When we withdraw into our Christian cocoons, we choose to isolate ourselves in a Christian subculture. We want to separate ourselves from evil influences, so we withdraw. Some use the analogy of Christian "islands" in a secular sea. I refer to this as a "fortress" mentality—building Christian castles and digging moats around ourselves to keep the world out. Staub uses the image of "circling the wagons to keep the 'good guys' in and the 'bad guys' out." Whatever the analogy we use, the result in outreach is the same: The only way that the community of faith grows is either biological or through an accidental seeker who comes into our world.

Posture #2: Combative. Those hostile to the world see themselves as the Israelites in the Promised Land—trying to cleanse the ground of the unholy and profane. Dean Merrill describes this "us" versus "them" mentality.[8] One illustration of the combative approach is the story of Fred Phelps. His "mission of hate" brought him to the funeral of a homosexual murdered in Wyoming in 1998 with signs reading, "God hates fags." Phelps is an extreme that most Christians would discredit, but the temptation we face in a society in moral decline is to withdraw more and more and enter it only in the spirit of hostile confrontation. Even allowing for the prophetic role of the church, a combative approach will seldom persuade people to consider God's redemptive love found in Jesus Christ.

Posture #3: Conforming. This is total identification. Christians conform to the values and behaviors of our society. We blend into secular society like chameleons, to the point where little to no difference exists between us and the world in terms of how our lives look and the values we live by.

Obviously, none of these negative responses help us as we attempt to reenter the world we're trying to reach. So how can we?

AT YOUR CORE: DEVELOP A HEART LIKE GOD'S

Why go into the world and build friendships? What motivates evangelism and outreach? What stirs us to leave our comfort zones in an effort to engage the world with the gospel message? Why do churches and individuals participate in evangelism—both locally and globally? Where does a sustained heart for the lost come from? I think about these questions a lot because I spend large amounts of time trying to influence people and churches to be more involved in outreach and cross-cultural missions.

Is evangelism simply obedience to the specific Great Commission of Matthew 28:18-20? Do we get involved simply because of needs that we see in people near and far? Are we interested in global missions because of the global village we now live in?

Christie and I were discussing these questions one night after dinner, and she offered the most succinct response. She said, "It's simple. We're involved to reflect the character of God. Missions is God's heart."

At the foundation of our desire to mobilize the local church for local and global outreach stands the character of God. As followers of Christ, we supremely desire that our lives and our churches reflect God's character to the world. We want a heart for the lost because God has a heart for the lost!

God reveals his character to us as he makes himself known in the Scriptures. We get a glimpse of God's character by looking at the questions he asks. Whether they're rhetorical (like the questions God asks Job) or instructive (like Jesus' "Who do you say that I am?" question to Peter), God uses questions as devices to teach us something about himself.

Consider three questions God asks that explain how his character lays the foundation for outreach, evangelism, and even cross-cultural missions. The questions reveal God's heart for lost people. God utters them to tell us how he looks at our broken world.

Foundation #1: Seeking lost things. God's first communication with humankind after sin entered the world came in the form of a question: "Where are you?" (Genesis 3:9).

This question, posed by God as he sought out Adam and Eve after their rebellion, tells us of God's seeking heart and that the loving Father pursues lost sinners. When they were afraid and hiding, God came looking. Because he's omniscient and omnipresent, he obviously knew where they were. So why did he ask, "Where are you?" Because God wanted Adam and Eve to know that—in spite of their flagrant sin and disobedience—he wanted the relationship to be healed. The offended came after the offender and said, in effect, "I want to redeem this relationship."

Jesus reflected that same priority through his stories in Luke of lost things being earnestly pursued: lost sheep, a lost coin, and a lost son. He summarized his passion for things lost to those who criticized his outreach to Zacchaeus: "For the Son of Man came to seek and to save what was lost" (Luke 19:10).

God comes looking for us. He wants to get us back into relationship with him, and *he* seeks after *us* (even though we broke the relationship). After he finds us, he calls us to imitate his heart by seeking others. We love because he first loved us. We seek because he first sought us.

When we follow Christ, he calls us to go into the world asking the same question to the broken world: "Where are you? God wants a restored relationship with you." The apostle Paul captured this spirit when he referred to us as "Christ's ambassadors" reaching out in reflection of God's seeking heart by urging people to "be reconciled to God" (2 Corinthians 5:20). If we understand the seeking heart of God, we'll find ourselves joining in the plea to others: "Be reconciled to God." The loving Father-God wants you back.

Bob understood this and joined a local athletic club in an effort to engage people by seeking those who know nothing of God's love. God's seeking heart motivated Debbie to decrease her activities at church in order to spend more time with her unchurched neighbors. God's seeking heart moved Joan to serve in an inner-city soup kitchen. In Fred, it resulted in establishing an "inquirers" Bible study at work. In Jim and Andrea, it resulted in a commitment to cross-cultural ministry in Central Asia with an unreached ethnic group.

Leith Anderson writes of a young family who came to faith because someone went looking for them:

One young mother came to a Mothers-of-Preschoolers (MOPS) weekday program at Wooddale Church because another mother in her neighborhood invited her. She had no church background and no religious interest. She simply had a friend and wanted to make more friends. MOPS was a positive experience. Her relationships multiplied and deepened. As Christmas neared she saw a poster in the church building advertising the annual Christmas concert. She and her husband liked good music, so they decided to attend. As they drove home that night, they decided that they had enjoyed the music. They decided that it would be good for them to raise their children in a church, something neither of them experienced growing up. Before they reached home they decided to join Wooddale Church and raise their children there — although they acknowledged to each other that they had no idea as to what kind of church it was or what the church believed and taught. Unusual? Probably not. More and more unbelievers first come to church because of relationships, not religion. They are most likely to adopt the beliefs and faiths of their friends.[9]

When we understand God's seeking heart, we always maintain an outward focus that thrusts us out into evangelism, mercy ministries, and cross-cultural outreach.

God seeks the lost—and so do his people who comprehend his heart.

Foundation #2: God's sacrificial heart. On the cross, Jesus uttered a question that revealed a second truth about God's heart. As he absorbed the weight of human sin and the wrath of God, he asked, "My God, my God, why have you forsaken me?" (Matthew 27:46).

These words reflect God's willingness to go to great lengths to win back lost people. God loves us so much that he comes and pays the price for the sins that we've committed (see Isaiah 53:6). This question informs us that Jesus suffered separation, loneliness, and pain so that he might make it possible for us to come back to God (see 1 John 4:10).

When we understand this sacrifice for our sins, God's love "compels us" (2 Corinthians 5:14) to sacrifice ourselves in order to reach others. We're willing to suffer inconveniences so that others can know the love of the God who gave himself for them. His sacrifice stirs us so that we no longer live for ourselves "but for him who died for them and was raised again" (2 Corinthians 5:15).

God's sacrificial heart motivates incarnational ministry. As Jesus left his comfort zone to serve us by his death on the cross (see Philippians 2:5-11), we in turn leave our comfort zones—to get the message of Christ's love out to the world.

Imitating the sacrificial heart of God leads to an integrated faith that touches the real issues of daily living. Integrated faith is authentic faith. We start grappling with how issues of faith apply to our modern world. As Christians, how do we respond to AIDS, racism, environmental issues, or euthanasia? What does it mean to be a Christian in a secular or pluralistic society?

An integrated faith and life expands our witness. When we address our perspectives and responses to human rights issues, economic injustices, and world hunger, people may be drawn to our Savior because they see the relevance of our faith to the real issues of the world.

God's sacrificial heart motivates a doctor to give up a lucrative career in plastic surgery to do cleft palate surgery in Zambia. God's sacrificial heart at work in Beth stirs her ministry with HIV/AIDS patients in Boston. Understanding God's sacrificial heart called Bruce and Karen to dedicate their lives to urban gang members. It also led Vivian to become a foster mother to two cocaine-addicted babies.

Look into the motivation of Christian refugee camp workers, Christian street workers in Calcutta, or generous people giving away large amounts of money to Christian ministry, and you'll almost always find God's sacrificial heart being reproduced in his children.

When we understand God's sacrificial heart, we build the foundation for sacrifices we need to do the work in the world of evangelism, mercy ministries, and cross-cultural outreach. God sacrifices to get the message of his love out—and so do his people who comprehend his heart.

Foundation #3: Living as "sent" people. God shows us his heart through a third question—this one asked of Isaiah the prophet: "Whom shall I send? And who will go for us?" These words, spoken to Isaiah before his famous response—"Here am I. Send me!" (Isaiah 6:8)—reflect God's sending heart. God sends us out to get the message of his love to the world.

Jesus commissioned his disciples to make more disciples (see Matthew 28:18-20), preach the good news everywhere (see Mark 16:15; Luke 24:45-49), and be his witnesses to the ends of the earth (see Acts 1:8). All these commands launch us out because Jesus said, "As the Father has sent me, I am sending you" (John 20:21).

We *are* God's method. He fully intends to involve us as his local and worldwide ambassadors; God makes his appeal of love and reconciliation to the world through us (see 2 Corinthians 5:20).

Chuck, a recent masters-level graduate working behind the counter at a fast-food chain, understands God's sending heart when he says, "This isn't where I'd choose to be right now, but God has me here—to touch people who might otherwise never know about the love of Jesus. I work with people from eleven nationalities; God has sent me into international missions right behind this counter."

Katie and Jack, Bible translators pioneering in Central Africa, understand God's sending heart when they state, "God could reach these people in any way he wants, but for some wonderful reason, he chooses to reach them through us."

When we understand God's sending heart, we start accepting our God-given privilege of partnering with him in outreach. We're the primary expressions of the love of God that people see.

God sends us to be his ambassadors—an awesome truth for those who comprehend his heart. Our dedication to local outreach and our motivation for global ministry flow out from this facet of the heart of God.

THE SENDING GOD PRODUCES AGENTS OF HOPE

Lesslie Newbegin, veteran of decades of missionary service in India, writes, "the distinguishing mark of [the Christian] community will be hope." [10] In a world suffocating in hopelessness or meaninglessness or despair, our mission in the world is to build hope and a sense of positive anticipation of the future. In response to this suffocation, we present Jesus as hope because this hope "is the oxygen of the soul." [11] We go into the world and build friendships around our Jesus-centered message of hope. We go into our workplaces, our neighborhoods, and across cultures to say to the world that God has a "hope and a future" for them (Jeremiah 29:11).

Vincent Donovan, author of *Christianity Rediscovered*, went as an agent of hope to the nomadic Maasai people of East Africa. Through many struggles and lessons in true cross-cultural adaptation, he lived and ministered with people who feared change of any kind, feared evil spirits, and feared death. Donovan observed that the Maasai demonstrate their unwillingness to deal with the future with the fact that their language has no future tense. Through presenting Jesus Christ and the hope of the present and the future, Donovan addressed their fears of change, evil, and death. He summarized, *"I think you could say that one of the purposes and goals of evangelizing the Maasai is to put a future tense in their language."* [12]

How do our actions in the gospel serve to "give people a future tense"? Zac Niringiye and the leadership of FOCUS, a college-age ministry in Uganda, live out their commitment to be Christ's agents of hope in a country devastated by the HIV/AIDS virus. He says, "Several years ago we decided that AIDS is not a social challenge; AIDS is a challenge to the church." [13] So FOCUS has established ministries to serve the families of those with HIV/AIDS. In spite of opposition—even from other Christians who thought the disease was "God's judgment on sinful behavior"—they moved forward.

They offer proactive public health prevention, counseling to grieving people, and support for the thousands of children orphaned by the disease's impact on their parents. They work to give their country a "hope and a future" through the demonstrated love of Jesus.

Let's get practical. How can we be "agents of hope" in the world we touch?

Practice #1: Make friends. I apologize for stating the obvious, but I think we forget. If we want to develop "close proximity" to unchurched people, we need to get to know them on their own turf, not just at church outreach events. And we need to get to know them as *friends*—not as targets or outreach goals.

We live in a perfect age for such an approach. Why? Because so many people live virtually friendless lives. Most people really want friends. They want to find a place like the bar on the TV show *Cheers*—where "everybody knows your name and they're always glad you came." For people who espouse a religious faith based on the communication of unconditional love, we couldn't ask for a more perfect context in which to minister.

How do we start?

- Join something that nonChristians participate in—neighborhood sports, local school activities, community associations (see more on this in Heart Builder #9).

- Take a class. For Christie and me, some of our best contacts for meeting people have come from taking a computer class, a tennis class, and Spanish class.

- Walk around the neighborhood. Meet some neighbors. And then have a neighborhood cookout or an apartment "block party" where you can meet people on neutral ground.

- Ask for help. Related to walking around the neighborhood, asking a neighbor to borrow something is a great way to "break the ice" and start a conversation.

- Look for common interests. Travel, kids, and gardening can all help start a friendship. Most of my conversations with the guys at the pool (who I now consider friends) started with discussions about common interests in sports.

- Get to know service people by name. The people who serve you at restaurants, cashiers in stores, the local police, people at the bank, people who service your car—they all have names! And speaking to them by name often sets you apart as a caring customer.

- Go back to the same people. Using the same mechanic, sitting at the same table at a local coffee shop, and using the same travel agent establish superficial friendships—but ones that you can develop further.

- Choose one or two people to pray for. God can open friendship doors that you've never dreamed of.

Practice #2: Open your eyes. The church where I formerly served has more than two thousand attendees on Sunday morning. Sundays vibrate with activity—big services, multiple programs, Sunday school classes, and more. It's an exciting place to be.

But living in that world, it became easy for me to think that the activity of the church reflects everyone's experience. One summer Sunday I had the day off—so we went to the beach. I was amazed when we got stuck in traffic about a mile from the beach parking lot. Hundreds of others were arriving at the beach about the same time—and it wasn't even 10:00 A.M. I turned to Christie and said, "Wow, a lot of people skipped church today!"

Christie looked back and replied, "Welcome to the real world." She works in a hospital laboratory surrounded by unchurched people. She continued. "Do you see all these people at the beach? They're just like the people I work with. Do you realize that in my lab of more than twenty workers I'm the only one who goes to any form of religious worship outside of holidays, weddings, and funerals? Open your eyes."

A heart for the lost means understanding that people don't even think about the things that preoccupy us. When we're involved in a host of Christian activities in our small groups or churches, it's easy to think that everyone in the world is just like us.

We need to take a break. Step back. Realize that in the worlds we touch (neighborhood, job, school) dozens of people *never* even think about God, *never* attend church, *never* wrestle with subjects such as "God's call" on their lives, and *never* wonder about heaven and hell.

When we open our eyes, the challenge to reach out gets bigger. We realize that our challenge isn't just to respond to people's spiritual questions. Instead, we need to build friendships and create an environment of trust where we can introduce people to questions they may have never considered.

Practice #3: Open your ears. As we seek to enter the secular world, we increase our effectiveness in building relationships and guiding conversations in a spiritual direction by listening to the things that concern others.

A woman sitting next to me on a flight across the country looked tense before we took off. I asked, "Are you all right?" She replied, "Well, no. You see, I fear flying because I'm just terrified of death." Her comment opened the door to a discussion about life and death, and I shared about my assurance of salvation in Jesus Christ.

Most listening, however, comes in more subtle forms:

- Watch the most popular movies or TV shows and form questions around these shows that you can ask coworkers or neighbors. When the television show *Touched by an Angel* was at the height of popularity, it stirred some interesting discussion about the supernatural. But even discussion about the TV show *X-Files* has helped me understand what people think about the supernatural world.

- Use popular music and the lyrics of songs. A long while ago, I asked some students "What are you living for?" by starting with a discussion of the song "Dust in the Wind"—where the group Kansas sings their despair over the fact that we're all just "dust in the wind." Listening to the discussion taught me about the hopelessness experienced by many young people.

- Use issues in the news. In our community, just asking the question "What do you think about the government allowing or disallowing school prayer?" stimulates good discussion. The replies of my friends give me insights into their opinions about religion and about prayer.

Relationships—listening—watching. All three increase my effectiveness as a witness and an ambassador for Jesus Christ. All three are possible when I'm outside of the community of faith developing "close proximity" with people God loves.

HEART BUILDER #7
SAY SOMETHING

In the past few months, I think I've heard a quotation attributed to Francis of Assisi (or at times, Mother Teresa) at least twenty times. It's a dynamic quotation, often cited in reaction to the preachiness of evangelical faith. The intention of the quote is to exhort listeners to make sure they understand that their lives are their greatest sermon.

The quote? "In all ways preach the gospel. If necessary, use words."

What a great exhortation! It often accompanies corollary statements such as, "One of ten people will read the Bible, but nine of ten will read the Christian."

These observations ring true, especially in our culture, where Christians often call up images of protests and meanness. But be careful that we don't react to one extreme by swinging to the other.

Lifestyle and obedience are of primary importance, but *words are important too*. We desire to live a Christlike life. Asking, "What Would Jesus Do?" influences our behavior. But without proclaiming Christ with our words, the world looks at us with admiration about what moral and compassionate people we are—without understanding *why* we are. Without an explanation, observers easily conclude that we're just exceptionally nice people.

Writing to the church at Rome, Paul exhorted Christlike living, godly character, and gracious behavior. But he also challenged the Roman Christians to witness verbally:

For, "Everyone who calls on the name of the Lord will be saved." How, then, can they call on the one they have not believed in? And how can they believe in the one of whom they have not heard? And how can they hear without someone preaching to them? And how can they preach unless they are sent? . . . Consequently, faith comes from hearing the message, and the message is heard through the word of Christ. (Romans 10:13-15,17)

So, Francis of Assisi not withstanding, let's recommit ourselves to the balanced witness of *both* life *and* word.

Evangelism isn't up to us. Evangelism is something that God does; we are only the instruments he uses. God's initiative precedes our response. God is always there first. — Rebecca Manley Pippert

HEART BUILDER #8:

REMEMBER—GOD'S
AT WORK BEFORE YOU

Develop the spirit of expectancy!

In a sermon entitled "Being Christ's Witnesses," a pastor started his challenge by outlining all of the obstacles we face—secularism, pluralism, other world religions, the postChristian mind-set of people, and a half-dozen other major barriers confronting us as aspiring witnesses for Christ. During this disheartening introduction, I leaned over to a fellow listener and whispered, "If he intends to discourage us from even trying, he's succeeding magnificently."

We all know the great challenges against developing and living out a heart for lost people, but if we focus only on the challenges, we'll miss the power of God. When we go into the world as witnesses, we can go with courage—in spite of the obstacles—because God goes before us.

A spirit of expectancy builds our heart for the lost world because it grows from the assurance that God is at work. Paul wrote to the Corinthians to underscore the work of God "behind the scenes" in every process of evangelism and conversion: "I planted the seed [of the gospel]. Apollos watered it, *but God made it grow.* So neither he who plants nor he who waters is anything, *but only God, who makes things grow....* For we are God's fellow workers" (1 Corinthians 3:6-7,9, emphasis added).

As followers of Jesus going into the world, we can be confident that God is already at work. Mark Acuff writes, "The 'lost' stories that Jesus told (Luke 15) made it clear that if we let Jesus be Jesus among us, there would be no shortage of response."[1]

God works through us, but he also works before us and after us. For that reason, we can live expectant lives. We can go into each day with a joyous anticipation and wonder, always asking, "God, how are you going to be at work in and through my life today?"

What can we expect?

EXPECTATION #1: GOD CAN USE ME

Ever feel insignificant? Too small to make a difference? Maybe we feel like the college student who was studying at a secular campus who told me, "My school and my area of study [sociology] is so liberal, I'm afraid to even mention that I'm a Christian. The challenge overwhelms me."

Sound familiar? Perhaps nothing will shrink our worldview faster than a sense of being overwhelmed by the "unChristianness" of our world—whether the global realities of need or just the values and attitudes we see every day. As limited humans, we want to shrink back like turtles into the protective shells of insignificance.

The sense of being overwhelmed reduces many Christians to silence. We maintain our personal faith, but we don't look for opportunities to live as witnesses. Our lives say, in effect, "I believe in God, but I doubt that he can use me or work through me."

However, Scripture reassures us that God wants his glory to be declared among the nations (see Psalm 96:3). We see his love for redeeming people, "not wanting anyone to perish, but everyone to come to repentance" (2 Peter 3:9; see 1 Timothy 2:4). And he calls us to be his witnesses to our community, across cultures, and even to the ends of the earth (see Isaiah 6:1-8; Matthew 9:36-38; Acts 1:8).

So here's the challenge: Do we believe in a personal God who uses broken, limited, and overwhelmed people to be his messengers to the world? Paul reminded the Corinthians that God does the miraculous work of using the limited and insignificant to change the world.

> Brothers, think of what you were when you were called. Not many of you were wise by human standards; not many were influential; not many were of noble birth. But God chose the foolish things of the world to shame the wise; God chose the weak things of the world to shame the strong. He chose the lowly things of this world and the despised things—and the things that are not—to nullify the things that are, so that no one may boast before him. It is because of him that you are in Christ Jesus, who has become for us wisdom from God—that is, our righteousness, holiness and redemption. Therefore, as it is written: "Let him who boasts boast in the Lord." (1 Corinthians 1:26-31)

As I've said earlier, in some miraculous and incomprehensible way, God uses you and me to work in the lives of the people around us. In these verses, God also affirms that he does his greatest work through the small, the humble, the lowly, and the insignificant.

The Corinthians wanted status. Paul the apostle wrote to them to affirm to them that God—in contrast to their drive for status—uses the least likely people to change the world. Why? So that the work done will clearly be seen as the work of God, that no one can boast except in the Lord (see verses 29-31).

So, if you see yourself as small, insignificant, or overwhelmed, take courage; you're exactly the humble type of person who God wants to use mightily in the world! I suggest five specific ways that God can and does use our lives. Consider them as they apply to God using us to love and touch our lost friends.[2]

1. God uses our availability. When the prophet Isaiah responded to God's question, "Whom shall I send. And who will go for us?" (Isaiah 6:8), he felt very unqualified. Only moments earlier he had confronted his own sinfulness and the sinfulness of his people. As a prophet, he realized that before God's greatness, even the thing he thought he could offer—his preaching—was worthless: "I am a man of unclean lips" (verse 5).

But after experiencing God's forgiveness, Isaiah replies with a spirit of availability. He says, "Here am I. Send me!" (verse 8). No presumptive attitude. "I don't know if I have anything to offer, Lord, but here I am—available and openhanded—at your disposal."

Remember the story of the boy with five loaves and two fish? Jesus' disciples faced an insurmountable task—feeding five thousand men (plus women and children). They didn't have the food, the money, or the resources. All they had was a little boy who made his lunch available to Jesus. Yet through him the crowd was fed (see John 6:1-13).

Will we give our limited resources to Jesus? Will we give him our fears, our sense of inability, our inadequacy in responding to tough questions? If we do, we'll find that he wants to use our lives.

Take this thought into this week: God uses ordinary people who make themselves available to him. On the drive to work: "Here am I. Send me!"; upon entering the warehouse or the office or the lab or the schoolroom: "Here am I. Send me!" Our job is to make ourselves available and then expect that God will work!

2. God uses our experiences. Jesus called four of his twelve disciples by using their profession as fishermen as his invitation. When he said, "Follow me . . . and I will make you fishers of men" (Matthew 4:19), he invited them to allow him to redeem their pasts for the sake of the kingdom of God.

"Did you develop patience as a fisherman? I'll use that for my kingdom. Did you devise strategies to run your business? I'll use that for my kingdom. Can you discern the weather and the seas? I want to use you to discern the times and the spirits." He was inviting them to allow him to use the skills and character traits that they had learned as fishermen for the purposes of God's kingdom. (my paraphrase and elaboration of Matthew 4:19)

Once, when speaking at a church service, I described my brother—who was then the president of a motorcycle gang. His external appearance testified of the culture he lived in—long hair, a bushy beard, tattoos, and black leather clothes. After the service, a man approached me. He had long hair, a bushy beard, a motorcycle-gang jacket, tattoos, and black leather pants. He said, "I've just gotten saved and I want to reach out to your brother. Maybe he'll listen to me."

The doctrine of the sovereignty of God affirms our belief that in "all things God works for the good of those who love him" (Romans 8:28). Throughout the course of our lives, God sends or allows a host of experiences that he can use for his purposes. When we combine availability with experiences, we say to God, "Here I am, Lord; how do you want to use my family background, my experiences growing up, my education, and my life background—to open the doors of Christ's kingdom to others you'll send me to?"

3. *God uses our prayers.* In Matthew 9:36-38, Jesus confronted overwhelming need—people who were "harassed and helpless, like sheep without a shepherd" (verse 36). He then noted the need for laborers in God's harvest field—people who can serve and speak and love these people.

If I faced what Jesus saw, I would have turned to the disciples and said, "So get out there, you guys, and meet those needs!" But Jesus started differently. He said to the disciples, "Pray." He told them to look upward. Ask the Lord of the harvest.

Prayer reminds us that God's in control. Prayer turns our attention away from the insurmountable needs to the almighty God, because for him, nothing's insurmountable. In light of the great distress of people and needs of the world, the disciples first needed to acknowledge through prayer that the Lord of the harvest was in charge.

In Christie's laboratory, she works with coworkers she's been a witness to for more than twenty years. She's invited some to church and others to special outreach functions. At this writing, none have come to faith in Christ. For more than twenty years, her motto has been, "Keep praying."

And she has. Just last month three mini-miracles happened. First, Christie has long prayed for a Christian coworker. When a new woman joined her team, within a week, Christie discovered that she had her first Christian coworker—her evangelistic team doubled!

Christie has prayed for the opportunity to articulate the gospel one on one to coworkers who knew she was "religious," but who didn't understand the idea of a personal relationship with God through Christ. A second coworker asked Christie to lunch last month. She wanted to find out from Christie "what she really believes," and Christie was able to articulate a clear presentation of the gospel.

A third coworker told Christie that her daughter had become a Christian. This woman asked Christie to take her through a Bible study so that she might understand the decision her daughter has made.

Expect that God will use your life—as you pray!

4. *God uses our pain.* Paul reminded the Corinthians that God comforts us in our afflictions so we might in turn "comfort those in any trouble with the comfort we ourselves have received from God"

(2 Corinthians 1:4). As we make ourselves available to God, he uses our difficulties, pains, disappointments, and suffering for his purposes.

The gospel message is all about how God used the pain of Jesus on the cross to complete the work of redemption. And God can use our pain likewise.

Errol had a powerful witness to alcoholics because he had himself been delivered from alcohol. The famous missionary Mary Slessor reached out and won many abused children to Christ—because she herself had come from an abusive, alcoholic home. As he lay dying of cancer in a hospital ward, Ernie's last prayer request was that he could testify boldly of Jesus Christ to those around him who were similarly dying. And Joni Eareckson Tada witnesses powerfully of the grace of Christ to those who are disabled—because she has been paralyzed from the neck down since the age of seventeen.

If we're convinced that we can't make a difference as witnesses because our painful pasts or our present difficulties disqualify us from bringing good news to others, we need to come back to the reality of Scripture. It clearly communicates that God can turn pain into his avenue of grace and mercy. Our pains—past or present—may be God-given avenues into ministries that we could never undertake pain-free.

5. *God uses our faith.* If we want to see God use our lives, we need to be willing to take some risks. Believing that God can use our lives to influence others involves faith, and faith involves risk. The great missionary pioneer to China, Hudson Taylor, said it best: "Unless there is an element of risk in our exploits for God, there is no need for faith."

Taking a risk regarding outreach takes different shapes. It might mean crossing over into a different cultural or racial section of the city in an effort to build friendships. It might mean stepping out in evangelical witness in the workplace. It might mean risking the ridicule or rejection of church friends as they criticize our desire to go into the world, befriend nonChristians, and cut back on our religious activities.

But Scripture and Christian history clearly illustrate that God uses people who step out in faith, leave their comfort zones, and take a risk that says, "God, I'll get involved if you give me the courage, strength, and endurance I need." And when we venture forward in risk-taking faith, God meets us there!

Reread Hebrews 11. In this listing of the "Hall of Fame" of faith, we find some pretty seedy characters. We meet murderers (Moses and David), liars (Abraham, Jacob, and David), a coward (Gideon), and some who gave in to their fleshly lusts (Samson, David, and Rahab). Is God encouraging us to imitate their weaknesses? Of course not! But he is reminding us that by faith, he can work past our defects.

The God who influenced Egypt through Joseph, Babylonia through Daniel, Nineveh through Jonah, and the world through Paul—this is our God! We may feel inadequate and overwhelmed, but our God chooses to work through the weak and the foolish. We have an *awesome* God, a God who will do his work through people like you and me!

EXPECTATION #2: GOD CAN USE MY WORDS

While we want to expand the idea of being witnesses (see Heart Builder #3), the truth remains that people hear the good news about Jesus Christ when someone else communicates it to them. Consider these words that Paul wrote to the Romans:

> But before people can trust in the Lord for help, they must believe in him. And before they can believe in the Lord, they must hear about him. And for them to hear about the Lord, someone must tell them. And before someone can go and tell them, he must be sent. It is written, "How beautiful is the person who comes to bring good news." But not all the Jews accepted the good news. Isaiah said, "Lord, who believed what we told them?" So faith

comes from hearing the Good News. *And people hear the Good News when someone tells them about Christ.* (Romans 10:14-17, *New Century Bible,* emphasis added)

God works through our words. People need to hear the good news, and "people hear the Good News when someone [that's you and me!] tells them about Christ." Note the chain of the verbs in these verses: trust—believe—hear—tell—sent. They highlight how people come to faith in Christ. To come to faith, people have to *trust* in the Jesus they've come to *believe* in. But calling and believing isn't possible unless they first *hear* the message from someone who *tells* (or communicates) it, because that person understands that he or she has been *sent* as a message bearer.

When we understand how people come to faith in Christ, we understand the need for our participation. Jesus Christ is proclaimed when one person tells another about the Good News of forgiveness, eternal life, and spiritual transformation.

New Testament scholar F. F. Bruce identifies Romans 10:14-15 as the foundation of "the worldwide proclamation of the Gospel":

Hence [based on verse 13 — "whoever calls upon the name of the Lord shall be saved"] arises the necessity of proclaiming the Gospel worldwide. People are urged to call on the name of the Lord and be saved; but they will not call on his name unless they have been moved to believe in him; they cannot believe in him unless they hear about him; they cannot hear about him unless someone brings them the news; and no one can bring them the news unless he is sent to do so.[3]

How will people hear? People hear about Jesus through a human witness—our witness. God's Spirit works through our words. That's God's plan.

William Carey, called the father of modern missions, once proposed to a group of ministers that they discuss the implications of the Great Commission—especially as it pertained to preaching Christ to those who had never heard of him. An older minister, John C. Ryland, retorted, "Young man, sit down. When God pleases to convert the heathen, he will do it without your aid or mine!"[4]

Carey disagreed. He later went to India and inspired many others to follow. He understood the Scriptures correctly—that God has appointed human involvement in proclamation of the gospel. According to Romans 10, every one of us is key to helping people hear the gospel.

God will act through his Word—communicated through us. This inspires our prayers and urges us to seek training. We depend on God to work, but we also seek to do our best to communicate the message clearly.

Neil Anderson, serving with the Wycliffe Bible Translators in Papua, New Guinea, tells of having the privilege of explaining the love of God for the first time to the tribal people he and his family lived with. As he explained the sacrificial love of Jesus Christ and his demonstration of God's love by dying in our place, the people were amazed. They responded in their mother tongue, "We are dying of the deliciousness of these words." They couldn't find words to express their gratitude as they came to understand the Cross, God's forgiveness, and the gift of eternal life!

God entrusts us with the most delicious words that human ears can ever hear: "For God so loved the world that he gave his one and only Son" (John 3:16)—and God promises to work as we relay these words to others. People hear the good news about Jesus Christ when someone else communicates it to them.

EXPECTATION #3: GOD IS PREPARING PEOPLE

I need to tell you that I'm not a great witness. I try, but I never seem to be as successful as others are. My only successes in winning people to

Jesus Christ have come through long-term friendships, a lot of prayer, and lengthy conversations.

Some people really do manifest the gift of being evangelists. When they speak, people immediately respond and invite Christ to be Lord of their lives. In my earliest Christian years, the ministry I trained with taught us to always be looking for divine appointments. They urged us to look at every interchange with people as a chance to share the gospel—whether riding on the bus, doing laundry, or eating in the lunchroom at work.

I remember my feelings of inferiority when I compared myself to enthusiastic evangelistic speakers, who would relay stories such as this: "As I was flying in today, I had the privilege of sharing my faith with six people on the plane. As I shared my faith with the people around me, I led the woman in 10-F and the guy in 12-C to the Lord."

Such opportunities never seemed to come to me, and I wondered if I was an inferior Christian. I've learned, however, that while we may not all be so successful, we can all go looking for divine appointments. Several years ago—at the beginning of December—I was starting the process of evaluating the year that was almost over. To my horror, I came to the realization that I'd gone for eleven months without sharing my faith one on one with anyone. I began praying for divine appointments.

The next week I was flying to meetings in Chicago from my home near Boston. It's about a two-hour flight—plenty of time to strike up a conversation—so I started to pray for the person I'd sit next to on the plane.

The day came and I went into it with a sense of anticipation. I got to the airport, checked in, and waited to board. I was looking around the waiting area at different people, praying for my divine appointment. *Is he the one? Is she?*

I got on the plane and sat down. There was one seat next to mine. I actually laid hands on it, praying for the person who would sit there.

No one came. I kept praying. The flight attendants began their final checks before take-off. Still no one. I began to feel rejected by the Lord. I thought, "Here I am, ready and available to be Christ's witness, and God doesn't want me to speak. No one is coming."

Just before the attendants closed the door, a businessman tore through it. He looked disheveled, his tie off to one side, and several bags crumpled under his arm. He was sweaty, obviously having run to make this connection, and he came toward me. I helped him stow his bags. He sat down next to me and immediately laid his head back—as if he wanted to go to sleep immediately. I kept praying, "Lord, keep this guy awake. Let this be my divine appointment today."

I let him catch his breath a little, and then I said, "How's it going?"

He looked over at me with sweat still dripping off his forehead. "Not so good," he replied. "I'm burning the candle at both ends, working harder and harder. My life is full of stress. My girlfriend just died of cancer, and I'm really asking what it's all worth. I'm really wondering about the meaning of my life."

Whoa! How's that for a divine appointment?

My co-traveler opened the door immediately to intense conversation, and we talked the entire flight—about his life, life and death, the meaning of life, the meaning of life in Christ, and the invitation of God to a loving relationship. Did I lead him to Christ, ordain him to ministry, and commission him to missionary work all before we got to Chicago?

No. But I planted a seed. I prayed with him. I gave him the names of several churches in his area where he could bring his questions and his needs. And I corresponded with him, sent him a Bible, and invited his questions. I prayed for a divine appointment, and God brought him! Who is your divine appointment today? Open your eyes to the opportunities before you.

HEART BUILDER #8
DIVINE APPOINTMENTS

As a newly committed follower of Jesus Christ in college, I jumped into activity on our secular campus with an organization devoted to outreach and evangelism. Although I reflect back now with some questions on their methods and training, one theme in the instruction lingers with me every day. They always encouraged us to go into the day expecting divine appointments.

This teaching comes from the example of Philip in Acts 8. Wherever he went, he looked for opportunities to serve, to preach, and to affect others for Jesus' sake.

As a deacon, he served the needs immediately before him. As an evangelist launched into an unexpected encounter with the Ethiopian eunuch, he looked for ways to encourage understanding and response to the good news about Jesus. As an itinerant minister, he reacted to being "beamed over" to Azotus by looking for new opportunities to preach to those who had yet to hear about Jesus Christ.

Philip exemplifies a believer in search of divine appointments. Rather than looking at interruptions and unexpected human encounters as inconveniences, he responded to them as opportunities sovereignly created by God.

In our desire to mobilize others for outreach, and to be mobilized ourselves, the divine-appointment principle transforms the way we enter each new day. The people we encounter—next to us on the bus, the neighbor in need, the driver in search of directions, the coworker in the next cubicle—become God-ordained opportunities to respond with the love of Christ. Our whole perspective on each new day changes when we see the people cross-ing our paths as divine appointments sent from God!

You are a Christian today because somebody cared.
Now it's your turn. — Warren Wiersbe

HEART BUILDER #9:

RESPOND
CREATIVELY

Don't be afraid to try something new.

James Engel, former sociology professor at Wheaton College and Eastern University, challenged the church more than a decade ago with the creation of the "Engel Scale." This scale illustrated that people are at various stages in their spiritual journeys, and, in contrast to many of our techniques, they may not fit the assumptions that we have about them. For example, rather than being "seekers," they may have absolutely no awareness of God. They're far more likely to know David Letterman's Top Ten List than they are to know the Ten Commandments.

The story I told in Heart Builder #5 about my friend Bill and his questions about God, God's love, and eternal life illustrates a person who couldn't comprehend the phrase "God loves you and offers you eternal life."

If we're going to reach out in the twenty-first century, we can't rely on 1950s methodologies or approaches. We must be like the men of Isacchar in 1 Chronicles 12:32, "who understood the times and knew what Israel should do."

We need to understand our times and then *be innovative* in deciding how to respond.

In what follows, I offer ten ideas that others and I have found innovative. Maybe you want to implement these, or revise them, or make your own list of creative approaches to enlarging a heart for the lost.

IDEA #1: GO FOR A PRAYER WALK

If God indeed works through our prayer, but we find ourselves fearful of how to get started, how about a prayer walk? This involves just walking through our neighborhoods, our workplaces, or our schools, and praying—for households, coworkers, or classmates.

Our church recognized that our reputation in the community had deteriorated as the church grew. We were known as "the church that causes traffic jams." Add this to the fact that we paid no taxes and you'll see why the local government saw us as takers rather than contributors to the community.

So we went to the City Manager and asked, "What can we do to serve the community?" He looked at us skeptically (I think he doubted that we were serious) and said, "I'll get back to you."

Three months later he called and reminded us of our desire to contribute to our community. He asked us to deliver more than seventeen thousand town directories to every household. He inquired, "Can you do it?" We said yes.

Our church is large, but it was still a challenge to martial more than two hundred volunteers to give a September Saturday to deliver these directories. We found the volunteers, and we decided to do something that our church had *never* done in its five-decade history. We made this practical service event into a prayer walk—praying for *every home* in our community as we walked. The service project/prayer walk opened new ideas and opportunities for community outreach, and we entered that fall with a new sense of anticipation of God working through us.

Prayer walking can get personal too. Christie periodically goes into her lab early so that she can stroll from workstation to workstation, praying over the microscopes and the people she knows who will work there. Joe does the same in his workplace, praying over every cubicle. Sandra gets to high school early on Mondays and prays over every locker on her hall.

Earlier, I confessed the difficulty Christie and I have had in reaching out to our neighbors. We still haven't had much success, but we did walk around the neighborhood and get the names of every family and household—so that our efforts at outreach can start with prayer.

IDEA #2: CREATE A SAFE ZONE FOR QUESTIONS

Bob and Betty Jacks have been wonderfully successful in reaching out to an old, gospel-resistant area of New England by opening their home. In their book, *Your Home a Lighthouse,* they describe how they invite people into discussions of faith where no question is labeled silly and no one is expected to have previous biblical knowledge. The safe zone allows people to wrestle with their own faith without pressure.

A humorist once observed that "people who want to share their religious views with you almost never want you to share yours with them." Creating safe zones communicates, "I want to listen." But this challenges us because, in the words of Tim Muehlhoff, we suffer from agenda anxiety—we're so anxious to get across all of our points that we fail to give the time needed to listen to the views of others.[1]

Creating safe zones might mean inviting unchurched friends to our homes to view the *Jesus* film or to visitor-oriented church activities. Then we create the safe zone by following these activities up with an opportunity to ask questions on anything said or done that the visitor didn't understand.

I built on this idea and invited a friend to come to church with pen and paper in hand. I asked him to write down every action, phrase, or idea that he didn't understand. He observed things like,

- "You assume that I know where to find things in the Bible."
- "I didn't know we were supposed to pray, but everyone looked down and closed their eyes—then I knew."
- "When you asked me to register my attendance, I immediately thought, 'Why? What will they do with that information?'"
- "The pastor obviously knew what he was talking about—but I understood less than half of it."
- "I was completely lost with all the singing."
- "There are no signs to anything—so I got the impression that only the insiders knew their way around. A visitor like me felt lost."

From his feedback, we learned a lot about just how visitor-*un*friendly we'd become.

IDEA #3: BRING YOUR HOPE TO THE FUNERAL HOME

Although George Hunter observed that secular people are thinking about life *before* death (quoted in Heart Builder #5), the reality of death does open doors for discussion. To illustrate this, Dick Staub cites research from the University of Chicago's National Opinion Research Center that revealed that only 16 percent of eighteen- to twenty-two-year-olds had any contact with organized religion, but 81 percent of them said that they were asking spiritual questions like, "What happens when I die?"[2]

Maybe the best occupation an aspiring evangelist could have is a funeral home director. For many people, their direct confrontation with the realities of death, eternity, and belief opens their hearts to consider the gospel message. If a friend loses a loved one, I make an effort to go to the wake or the funeral—both because it teaches me how he or she views death and because it builds into a friendship a connection that I can follow up with later. Most people refer to the deceased as "going on to a better place," but there's seldom any basis for this and certainly none of the assurance of a Christian funeral.

Two summers ago, one of my Noon Platoon swimming friends (see appendix B) saw me in town. He said, "Are you going to be in town for the next few weeks? My mother's dying, and you're the only religious person I know. Would you do her funeral?" (He knew that I'm a minister.) I agreed immediately.

But after agreeing, I found myself saying, "What have you done? You never knew his mother and to your knowledge she has no faith of any kind."

About eight days later, his mother died. Christie and I stayed with our friend for the wake, the funeral, the graveside service, and the family gathering after the services. At the funeral, I preached a sermon entitled "Why Are We Here?" I explained that we're here to remember the deceased, and I delivered her eulogy. Then I observed that we're also here to comfort the family in their loss.

And then I said, "Why are we here? The third reason is to ask the question, 'Why are we here?'—not at this funeral specifically, but on this planet. We confront death, and it forces us to ask the meaning of life. Why indeed *are* we here?" I went on to explain God's view of the meaning of life as explained in the Scriptures, and I gave an overview of his invitation to a relationship with him—now and forever.

I didn't give an invitation; funerals aren't a time to exploit people's sorrow. I didn't make any official eternal diagnoses about the deceased (other than to release her to God's mercy). I only wanted to confront my listeners with the realities of death in hopes of launching them on spiritual searches.

You probably don't preach many funeral services. But don't lose the opportunity; death provides us with an open door to gently provoke people toward spiritual evaluation.

IDEA #4: PRACTICE HANDS-ON INVOLVEMENT

A. Skevington Woods is credited with observing, "The temptation of this pragmatic age is to presume that technique is the secret of evangelism."[3] We might fall prey to the same thought—if only I had training, a better "how-to" book, or a better technique, then I'd be a witness.

As helpful as technique can be, maybe we just need to start by serving practical needs as an avenue to communicate the love of Christ. The New Testament writer James challenges us to "show [our] faith by what [we] do" because "faith without deeds is dead" (James 2:18,26).

The apostle John began one of his letters by explaining the dramatic impact of his firsthand encounter with Jesus Christ: "That . . . which we have *heard*, which we have *seen* with our eyes, which we have *looked at* and our *hands have touched*—this we proclaim" (1 John 1:1, emphasis added). The verbs I italicized illustrate his practical encounters with the works of Christ.

Hands-on involvement works two ways as we look for ways to reach out. First, it adds credibility to the faith we profess to the world. That's why many nonChristians point to Mother Teresa's "Sisters of Charity" as the best example of true Christianity. To outside observers, who seldom care about doctrinal issues, these compassionate sisters' care for the poor authenticates Christian faith. One person—who knew little of what Jesus taught—told me, "They live the Christian life the way that Jesus exemplified."

Second, hands-on involvement invites the participation of nonChristians who have hearts of compassion. I asked a friend, "Would you be willing to come to church with me?" He said no, but then went on, "But I'll go with you to build homes with Habitat for Humanity." He wanted to serve. Practical care for those in need can invite people into the kingdom of Christ through action that leads to faith.

True faith takes shape in practical deeds of grace. The genuine experience of faith results in action. We get out and do something! In this "been-there, done-that" generation, action is critical. Don't just talk about the homeless; serve at a soup kitchen. Praying for international students isn't enough; have someone over to the house. Francis Bacon said, "It's not what we preach or pray, but what we practice that makes us Christians."[4]

IDEA #5: GETTING INVOLVED WITH THE POOR

This is a specific action related to Idea #4. Certain verses in the Bible exist to rattle our cages. They explode off the page to wake us up and cause us to reevaluate our actions. Jesus' words about the separation of the sheep and the goats in Matthew 25:31-46 certainly qualify. The Lord awakens his followers to the real definition of the gospel by explaining that God's judgment will be based on how we cared for people in need.

He reminds us that a visit to a prisoner, compassion to the impoverished (the giving of food to the hungry, drink to the thirsty, and clothes to the naked), and a visit to the lonely reflect our true love for him. If we are the people of Christ, we're supposed to be characterized by hospitality to the outcast and outreach to the poor. Omitting these practices results in eternal judgment. Sounds harsh, but it accurately portrays Jesus' concern that our faith touches people who are disadvantaged.

Jesus tells us that the genuineness of our faith, our outreach, and our Christlike love can be evaluated with one question: How does our faith take expression in caring for the poor? The observing world asks a similar question: "How does your Christianity demonstrate itself in your outreach to the poor?"

Ron Sider, professor at Eastern Baptist Seminary and founder of Evangelicals for Social Action, rocked the Christian world twenty years ago with his book *Rich Christians in an Age of Hunger*. He recently began challenging Christians to pragmatic ministry to the poor by joining in a covenant he calls the "The Generous Christian Pledge."[5] He encourages every Christian to undertake a lifestyle mission for the poor.

The cage-rattling statements of Jesus demand a response. The Generous Christian Pledge gets us started. If we live lives characterized by this compassion for the disadvantaged, the world will notice.

IDEA #6: LOOK CROSS-CULTURALLY—RIGHT WHERE YOU LIVE

One of the reasons we need to be creative in our efforts at reaching out to the lost stems from our changing world. Writing of the changing communities facing the North American church, Christian radio host and founder of The Center for Faith and Culture, Dick Staub, observes,

> The truth is, America's melting pot no longer (if it ever did) produces a uniform stew. Nose rings, language, dress, musical taste, even volume can be reflections of cultural differences found coexisting in most American cities. On our Naperville [a suburb of Chicago] street, you'll find recent immigrants from China, India, and Pakistan. You'll find first-generation Irish and Italian. There are those raised in urban Chicago living next to those raised on rural Illinois farms living adjacent to those whose only experience is upscale suburban living. In America our everyday encounters are increasingly cross-cultural.[6]

So what do we do—especially when we consider that many of these cross-cultural people live outside the reach of our normal circles of friends?

Consider starting ESL (English As a Second Language) classes in the church or community. It's a practical way to welcome first-generation people from other cultures and help them in very practical ways.

Get to know your community. I went to the local high school and asked them how many students they had in ESL programs. I wanted to see how international we were becoming. In a suburban community, in a high school with fewer than 2,000 students, *more than 160* were in the ESL program, representing *42 languages*—from Chinese and Korean to Hindi (India) and Wolof (Senegal, West Africa).

Host a World Religions class at church. When we did this, more than seventy people attended. When asked why they were taking the class, all gave the same reply: "I work with people from another major world religion, and I want to understand what they believe before I attempt to communicate Christ to them."

Look through the phone book. A former missionary to Pakistan, now living in Newark, New Jersey, taught us this. He looks through the phone book for Muslim names and then sends them invitations to dinner! Following his example, a first generation American from Sri Lanka in our church went through the community phone book and looked for names he identified as Asian or South Asian. He called these people and invited them to an international luncheon.

Invite to your home an international student who recently immigrated. He or she needs to know that the lifestyle depicted on TV doesn't represent every American home. Sadly, many international visitors (who arguably make up some very lonely and open-to-the-gospel people) never do see an American home—much less a Christian home.

IDEA #7: JOIN SOMETHING (OTHER THAN THE CHOIR!)

Innovative church planter Mark Acuff, whose effective outreach helped start a church in an area north of Boston, tells the story of how his relationship with a neighbor named Paul changed their church:

> The first several months [after we started our church], we attracted mostly unhappy members from other churches. That all changed when I met Paul through a youth basketball program. We each had a son on the team. As I got to know Paul, he asked me about church and said that he might come. He did, and for the next several months he and his wife examined and challenged everything about faith. When he finally submitted to the lordship of Christ, it was dramatic. He was so excited that he invited his neighbors, co-workers, and friends to church. Suddenly we were surrounded by "sinners." Paul and that experience became the new pattern, not the exception for our ministry.[7]

Acuff goes on to describe how the church requires that every church leader have some type of community involvement—from coaching youth soccer to being a member of the board of the local library.

Well-known author C. S. Lewis gave the metaphor describing Christians as the "carriers of the good infection." Others refer to Christians as "yeast" in society—with a permeating impact that causes morality and spirituality to rise. Whatever our analogy, the message is clear: Our maximum influence for Jesus Christ comes through involvement in the world we're trying to touch.

So join the PTA. Run for the school board or for city council. Get involved in the gardening club. Build relationships through local sports activities, through helping out with Boy Scouts or Girl Scouts, or through joining the local Chamber of Commerce. Become a volunteer. Offer to pray with the police. Host a neighborhood open house. Permeate your culture.

IDEA #8: PERFORM AN INTEGRITY TEST

What do we do when we have long-term relationships with nonChristians, and yet they never seem to respond to the gospel? Appendix A discusses the significance of long-term prayer (although written about praying for family members, it applies to friendships as well), but can we do more?

One exciting (and scary) idea I call an "integrity test." Christie and I have both tried it. We go to our nonChristian friends and ask them to evaluate our lives as followers of Christ. We ask questions like the following:

- "If I'm supposed to be salt, is there anything about my life that makes you thirsty to know God?"
- "You know me pretty well. Am I a good advertisement for following Jesus?"
- "Do you see any hypocrisy in my life that keeps you from wanting to consider Jesus?" (This is by far the scariest question; we pray that we respond with grace, not defensiveness.)

Christie and one coworker have known each other twenty-two years. When Christie invited her response to these and other questions, her friend (whose sister *has* become a Christian) replied, "I know how to become a Christian, but I just can't see myself ever doing what you've done because I'm not willing to be obedient. I don't want to submit to Jesus Christ as my Lord." The integrity test indicated that she at least knew the issues.

One of my friends—whom I've been building a relationship with for twelve years—replied, "I just don't see you as being that different from me, except that you're involved a lot at church." I asked, "How would you expect me to be different?" He had no specifics, but his answer provoked a lot of self-searching for me.

IDEA #9: ADDRESS FELT NEEDS

Our Christian witness often assumes that a person's first sense of need concerns his or her relationship with God. We ask questions like, "Don't you feel a spiritual void in your life?" When the person says, "No," we're stumped. We know theologically that people *should* feel a need for God, but they might not feel it.

Instead of addressing the gospel to what *we* think they need, why not start with what *they* feel they need?

- I shared one of Phil Yancey's books *Where Is God When It Hurts?* with my friend whose son had died at age ten. I said, "Would you take a look at this and tell me what you think?" It provoked some good discussion, and I communicated to him that I cared about the grief in his life.

- One church started Saturday breakfast seminars where people could come for a nice meal and then hear an expert speak to the issues that concerned them. The topics included investments, how to handle conflict at work, and managing stress in light of technology. People came and discovered that biblical truth actually spoke to their real-world issues.

- Many churches offer excellent programs for young children. Often, they attract neighborhood parents because even secular parents sense a need to educate their children with some sort of moral foundation.

George Hunter writes, "More and more preChristians will be reached through *small groups* or through *outreach ministries*—such as interest groups, support groups, recovery ministries."[8] Sports ministry, men's ministry, women's ministry, and a host of other specializations through our churches and evangelistic endeavors can debunk the secular idea that Christian faith is irrelevant. By speaking to the real needs of people, we provide foundations of credibility to challenge their deepest need—a relationship with God through Jesus Christ.

IDEA #10: SPEAK LOUDLY ABOUT JESUS

Throughout this book, I've steered clear of types of evangelistic methodologies that come across as insensitive and rude. So where does the idea that we should speak loudly about Jesus come from?

In the days of Soviet occupation of Eastern Europe, author and pastor Stuart Briscoe visited Poland. After he was met at the airport by two pastors, they all boarded the train that would take them to the pastors' village. After boarding the train, the pastors distanced themselves from Briscoe. After they were about ten feet from him on either side, one of the pastors said, "Brother Stuart, speak loudly of Jesus."

In that country, the government forbid street preaching, so the Christians had devised a plan that whenever they were traveling on public transportation, they would separate from each other and then loudly carry on their Christian conversations—implicitly inviting the bystanders to listen in.

"Speaking loudly of Jesus" doesn't grant me a license to be obnoxious. But it keeps me very aware of the fact that someone else might be listening in. At the locker room, I'll respond to someone's question, "How was your trip?" by giving a report of the state of the Christian church in places like Cuba or Pakistan. As a result of my travels, my swimming buddies know more about the church in Africa, Asia, and Latin America than they do about the church in our community.

If I get into a spiritual discussion with someone sitting near me on the bus, train, or plane, I quickly and silently pray for the others who might be listening in. In a restaurant, on a phone call, or in a shopping mall, I'm alert to the fact that others might be listening to the conversations I'm involved in. As a result, I speak loudly of Jesus with the hope that passive listeners might accidentally get a seed planted.

GLOBAL VILLAGERS—LIKE IT OR NOT

Old Testament prophets and poets exhorted God's people to think beyond themselves. The people of Israel suffered from ethnocentricity—the belief that the world (and their "tribal God") revolved around their ethnicity or nationality.

The psalmist wrote, "Declare his glory among the nations" (Psalm 96:3) to highlight the fact that God rules the earth; he's not some tribal deity for Israel's exclusive benefit. The prophets reminded readers that they were created to be a "light for the Gentiles" in order to "bring my salvation to the ends of the earth" (Isaiah 49:6). Beyond their cultural restraints, they attempted to mobilize God's people for outreach, acts of compassion, and cross-cultural missions.

We face the same task—to enlarge people's view of God and themselves as the people of God at work in the world. People resist actively ("I'm facing too many needs here") or passively (applauding our enthusiasm with no personal response).

To stir people to think about our global commission as followers of Christ, I start a sermon or Sunday school lesson by stating, "You're part of the Global Village whether you like it or not." To illustrate, I ask listeners to find another person and turn down the back collar of his or her shirt or blouse to see where the clothing was made. In a group of twenty-five people, the labels represent ten or twelve countries. Then we take ten minutes to pray for these countries (including our own)—for the strengthening of the church and the effective witness of God's people.

It's a small action, but it serves as an effective antidote to ethnocentricity—reminding us that we're called to declare God's glory to the nations.

I'm convinced that sharing our faith, regardless of the response,
is a key to our own spiritual health. —Mack Stiles

THE END RESULT:

CHANGED
LIVES

A heart for the lost changes us!

I pray that you may be active in sharing your faith, so that you will have a full understanding of every good thing we have in Christ. (Philemon 6)

Living with a heart for lost people bears fruit. As a result of our witness, people come to faith in Jesus Christ and his eternal family enlarges. Our lives, lived out as the salt of the earth and light of the world, serve as catalysts for others in their journeys of faith. Our heart for lost people brings outward, tangible change in the lives of others.

But our heart for the lost affects us inwardly too. That's why Paul prayed that Philemon would be "active in sharing [his] faith." Paul knew that living with an outward focus leads followers of Christ to a deeper personal relationship with God. As we look outward and seek after lost people who matter to God, he affirms and rewards us with growth, "so that [we] will have a full understanding of every good thing we have in Christ."

In addition to the obvious belief that people need a saving relationship with Jesus Christ (the objective rationale behind our witness), I advocate an active lifestyle of witness because of what it does for me and my faith (a subjective rationale). As God grows my heart for a lost world, I see four specific areas of growth in my own life.

GROWTH AREA #1: I DISCOVER THE GOSPEL AFRESH

In my earliest experiences of church, I remember songs with refrains like "Tell me the old, old story" and "Sing them over again to me, wonderful words of life." In my church, we seldom sing these songs any more. But their message still rings true. We tell the redemption story again and again because of what it does *for us.* In a sense, recounting the message of redemption, forgiveness, and new life in Christ helps me to get "saved" all over again (in an *experiential* way, not a *theological* one).

In heaven, the worshipers who now find themselves in the presence of God and free from the effects of sin still review the gospel story as part of their worship: "You are worthy to take the scroll and to open its seals, *because you were slain, and with your blood you purchased men for God* from every tribe and language and people and nation" (Revelation 5:9, emphasis added).

When I review the basic gospel message, I remember:
- that God loves and forgives *me.*
- that Jesus died on the cross to pay the penalty for *my* sins.
- that Jesus absorbed the judgment *I* deserve.
- that *I* have been born again by his Spirit.

In one conversation, I was sharing my own story of how I came to faith in Christ. I got so caught up remembering that amazing night when I first understood God's grace and forgiveness that I forgot about my listener. He asked, "Are you all right? You have a really distant look in your eyes."

I came back to the conversation, but my spirit gained new strength as I recalled that I was, am, and will always be a sinner saved by the grace of God through Jesus Christ.

Some outside of the Christian faith accuse us of being prideful, holier-than-thou types who talk down to people not like us. If we really listen to our own message, we'll be delivered from any such pride. The message of salvation—as we hear it again and even as we declare it—reminds us of God's great grace and mercy toward us.

GROWTH AREA #2: I GET INVIGORATED AS I SEE GOD TRANSFORM LIVES

Because of our work in the church and in missions, Christie and I have had the privilege of seeing lives transformed. We've heard the testimonies of drug addicts who were miraculously delivered from addiction and others who've received the strength to go through painful withdrawals. We've seen marriages saved and families healed. We know some people God delivered from destructive lifestyles and others who came to know Christ just before the destruction caught up with them. We've seen HIV/AIDS patients who gain a new hope in life and others who've gained a new confidence to face death.

Seeing and hearing about transformed lives invigorates me. It brings me back again to the personal, life-changing power of Jesus Christ. I remember the Saturday afternoon that my brother-in-law, Bob, trusted the Lord. After years of prayer (see appendix A) and diligent witness, he said, "Yes, I'd like to dedicate my life to Jesus Christ."

The only thing that exceeded our delight in seeing our prayers answered for his conversion was watching God transform his life over the next months. His countenance and his attitude changed. His relationships changed. His priorities changed. His demeanor toward others changed. And his purpose for living became full and other-centered. All of the changes didn't occur at once, of course, but the change was consistent and progressive. Watching the Spirit remake him revitalized us!

GROWTH AREA #3:
I GROW IN MY COMPASSION FOR OTHERS

As I grow to see others with the compassion of Christ, I may grieve to see the effects of sin, but I also see the redemptive possibilities in every person. Compassion means that I can't categorize people according to greater or lesser sins. The wild-living homosexual and the tax-evading middle-class manager and the pompously pious religious person—all are lost without Jesus Christ.

Several years ago, I preached at our church, and my then thirty-something-year-old brother told me he was coming to hear me. It was the only time other than our dad's funeral that he had been to church since he was eighteen. On the Saturday beforehand, I talked with him. I said, "Don't worry; I won't embarrass you by introducing you and asking you to stand." (Ours is a congregation of more than a thousand people.)

He surprised me with his response. He said, "No. Go ahead. Introduce me." He was daring me. My brother knew that his long hair, black, motorcycle-gang clothes, and tattooed arms weren't the norm for our church. Being convinced that our church was probably full of hypocrites, he wanted to prove that the church would feel awkward with his presence.

So, before the sermon, I introduced him. He stood and people clapped. After church, he was almost an hour late to lunch. "What happened to you?" we asked.

He said, "I was enjoying my newfound celebrity status." More than a hundred people had lined up to welcome him to church—from suited business executives to guys his age with long hair and tattoos to old church ladies he expected scorn from. I was proud of our congregation that morning—because they related to my brother with compassion. They saw him only as a sinner loved by Jesus.

Changing the way that I look at others (Heart Builder #2) expands my compassion. God sees no one as too far gone for his reach. The derelict on the street and the self-satisfied executive and myself—we all stand equal before God: equally sinful, equally loved, and equally in need of redemption through Jesus Christ.

GROWTH AREA #4:
I GET REVITALIZED IN MY OWN RELATIONSHIP WITH GOD

Like the church in Ephesus referred to in the book of Revelation, I find it easy to lose my first love (see Revelation 2:1-7). I may faithfully go through the motions of following Christ, but my heart grows cold or weary or stale.

A heart for lost people revitalizes me. It stirs me to grow. It reawakens my spiritual senses. It draws me back to the God who loves me. InterVarsity staff worker Mack Stiles writes,

> I'm convinced that sharing our faith, regardless of the response, is a key to spiritual health. Yes, of course we want to be effective in our witness. Yes, many Christians do dumb things that hinder the Gospel message . . . and we should take steps to change those things. But if we want to understand the riches of Jesus more deeply, we still need to be active in sharing our faith.[1]

If the lostness of people without Christ and the love of God for all people is still not enough to motivate us to grow a heart for the lost, then at least we can do it to provoke our own growth. We benefit. A heart for the lost transforms us.

THE END RESULT
THIS IS THE DAY OF GOOD NEWS

Many of us fail as witnesses simply because we don't speak up. We don't open our mouths because we fear social rejection. We resist the sense of urgency because we think, "Well, there will always be another time." We talk ourselves out of verbal witness because we imagine hearing questions that we don't know the answers to. And our real and imagined sins silence us, leaving us with the vague hope that our lifestyles alone will attract people to Jesus Christ.

As the "salt-of-the-earth," "light-of-the-world" people of God, our life examples serve as powerful witnesses. But there's more. An obscure story about four lepers (found in 2 Kings 7:3-11) offers some inspiration. In this story (first mentioned in Heart Builder #2), the people

of God are under siege. Four lepers decide that they'd rather die trying to find food than die in the besieged city.

When they venture out, they find the enemy camp deserted. To their amazement, the armies have fled and left the camp intact. They eat and they drink, and then they carry out their own personal plundering.

But then, together, they realize that their selfishness isn't good: "This is a day of good news," they observe, "and we are keeping it to ourselves" (verse 9). So they go and report the news. The news gets passed around with loud shouts in the city, and their report goes up to the palace. The rest of the story reveals that not everyone responded to their report; the lepers simply declared it.

We can apply the lesson of the four lepers as we seek to be witnesses of Jesus Christ, who is the *best* news of all. (I ask for a little indulgence from biblical scholars as I diverge into a more allegorical application of the text.)

- They were desperate. Are we? Or are we simply casual—both about our needs before God and the needs of the world we touch?
- They were part of a community under siege. Many of us see the Christian church this way—surrounded by "the world" but fearful of venturing out.
- They took a risk, which involved leaving their safety zone, risking their lives, and venturing out. Few of us risk our lives—but we're still afraid just to enter the world.
- They discovered that God had already gone before them—by confusing and scattering the enemy. When we venture out, we discover the same truth.
- They realized together that they had good news to share. Many times it takes a community discovery to enable us to take correct action.
- They risked social rejection by reporting their good news. After all, they were lepers—social outcasts.
- The entire community received their message of good news, even though not everyone responded in faith.

So then, in a world besieged by the spiritual captivity of sin, don't be silent. This *is* the day of good news. Don't keep it to yourself!

BIBLIOGRAPHY

Rather than just a random bibliography on all sorts of books related to evangelism and outreach, I thought I'd offer the books that have had the greatest impact on my heart for the lost.

Vincent Donovan's *Christianity Rediscovered* (Orbis, 1978) focused my attention on the priority and simplicity of conversion. The author describes his experiences as a missionary to the nomadic Maasai people of East Africa. His encounter with them and their encounter with the gospel forced me to ask, "How much of my views on evangelism comes from my Christian subculture—rather than from the Bible?"

George Hunter III's *How to Reach Secular People* (Abingdon, 1992) taught me how to understand people before trying to address the gospel to them. It also confronted me with my worldview—because I found that I was living with a "secularized" worldview rather than a biblical one.

Bill Hybels and Mark Mittelburg's book *Becoming a Contagious Christian* (Zondervan, 1994) (and seminar, tapes, and videos) was the first to challenge me toward a vital relationship with Christ that can overflow into evangelism. Their principle of "close proximity" challenged me to build some friendships with those outside of the Christian family. Check out *Building a Contagious Church* (Zondervan, 1997) too.

Robertson McQuilkin's *Great Omission* (OM Literature, 1999) really forced me to wrestle with the question about people being lost. The book investigates five reasons why we have not completed Christ's Great Commission. In the chapter on the "Wider Hope" theory, he confronts my inaction as a reflection of a disregard for the reality of the exclusiveness of Christ and eternal judgment.

Lesslie Newbegin's experiences as a veteran missionary to India inspired two books that taught me to look at my own culture with missionary eyes. *Foolishness to the Greeks* (Eerdmans, 1986) addresses the gospel in Western culture, and *The Gospel in a Pluralistic Society* (Eerdmans, 1989) challenges us to evangelize and dialogue with our diversified society.

Rebecca Manley Pippert's *Out of the Salt Shaker and Into the World* (InterVarsity Press, 1999) remains one of the best inspirational and practical tools on evangelism as a way of life.

OTHER RECOMMENDATIONS

Tim Downs's *Finding Common Ground* (Moody, 1999) serves as a good resource on learning to dialogue and sowing seeds rather than being preoccupied with "closing the deal."

InterVarsity Christian Fellowship's evangelism department has created a *GIG Guide*—with GIG meaning "Group Investigating God"—as a new model to train people in leading an evangelistic Bible study.

John Kramp's *Out of Their Faces and into Their Shoes* (Broadman and Holman, 1995) serves to help the reader "understand spiritually lost people and give them directions to God."

Jim Petersen's *Living Proof* (NavPress, 1989) comes as another highly recommended resource on sharing the gospel in the natural context of daily life.

Rick Richardson's *Evangelism Outside the Box* (InterVarsity, 2000) focuses on telling the "old, old story" in new ways to a postmodern generation.

Lee Strobel's *The Case for Christ* (Zondervan, 1998) is a fresh and helpful apologetic resource.

DON'T GIVE UP

ON YOUR FAMILY

Five Lessons We've Learned
About Praying for Lost Relatives

by Christie and Paul Borthwick

Then Jesus told his disciples a parable to show them that they
should always pray and not give up. (Luke 18:1)

One of the easiest areas to give up or "lose heart" (NASB) as we pray concerns our unsaved relatives. Our family members might be the people we
most earnestly desire to come to personal faith in Christ, but they simul-
taneously are often the people most resistant to our evangelistic efforts.
Most of us come to the point with our unbelieving relatives where all we
can do is pray. But prayer is tough. Prayer is hard work. It's long-term. And
prayer doesn't reduce itself to a neat and tidy formula of cause and effect.

OUR STORIES

We come from very different religious backgrounds. Christie came from
a religious family, but it was religiousness without a personalized
Christian faith. She came into a personal relationship with Jesus Christ
in her freshman year of college. She fervently desired that her family
would come to a similar personal faith, and she immediately became a

prayer warrior for her family. Her brother became a Christian after fifteen years of Christie's prayers and witness. Her mother trusted Christ nineteen years after Christie began praying. And her father called on the mercy of Christ at age eighty-three, twenty-nine years after Christie's prayers for her family members began.

On the other hand, I came from a strong, somewhat legalistic, Christian family. My two siblings and I actively rejected the faith as young teenagers. I repented and came to faith at age seventeen, but my brother and sister, who continued in their rejection of Christian faith, stopped attending church when they were eighteen. They remain people who are still spiritually "in process." I have prayed for my siblings since my conversion at seventeen, but without the kind of results Christie saw with her family. There's been very positive movement toward faith, but nothing conclusive — at least not yet!

We tell our stories because we've been learning the following lessons over the past thirty years as we've prayed for our relatives. We want to underscore from the outset that we don't have some sort of guaranteed formula to offer. Instead, by sharing what we've learned, we hope to encourage you regarding prayer for your family members. Keep praying and don't lose heart.

FIVE LESSONS

From our own experiences and from listening to the positive and negative experiences of others, here are the five most significant lessons we've learned about praying for family members to come to saving faith.

Lesson #1: Pray *for* your relatives, not against them. When we pray for family members who actively or passively reject the faith, it's easy to concentrate our prayers on issues related to their behavior. Because we live close to these folks, we see behaviors close up that irritate or aggravate us. Our relatives' swearing influences our kids; or their chain-smoking stinks up our houses and leaves a lingering smell in our furniture. Or perhaps their materialism taints the true meaning of Christmas, and their drinking mars family holidays—so we pray, "Lord, please bring them to yourself and make them stop."

This is especially true when Christian parents pray for their rebellious children. We're tempted to pray first for behavior modification: "Lord, please clean up his mouth," or "Make her stop smoking," or "Tell them to fix their marriage."

We know that conversion involves many life and lifestyle-changing transformations, but we've learned (the hard way) that God's *first* concern is for their salvation—life change precedes behavioral change.

In my own family, my well-meaning but overbearing father put a lot of pressure on his children, reminding us constantly that he was praying for us to "come back to the Lord." But this came across to us kids as "I'm praying that you'll come back to the Lord so that you'll clean up your act and stop embarrassing me in front of my Christian friends."

In his early years of young adult rebellion, my brother got the most pressure from our father concerning issues related to behavior. This pressure served to drive him further from Christ and the church. After Dad's death, Mom adapted a totally different tact. She prayed that her rebellious son would experience the unconditional love of Christ. She welcomed him to be with her in *any* context—including church and social settings where judgmental Christian friends would see her. She wanted her son to know that she loved and accepted him—tattoos, long hair, motorcycle, and all. And her unconditional love dramatically contributed to the softening of my brother's heart.

Lesson #2: Pray for patience; God's timing is seldom ours. Years of praying for unsaved relatives have taught us to look back and evaluate what we did right and where we failed. In her early Christian life,

Christie dragged her parents to multiple Christian meetings and services, thinking, "You know, God, this would be a perfect time for my parents to become Christians."

But they never did. So she persevered. She never stopped opening the doors where she could share her life and her faith. She never stopped including them in her spiritual journey. She introduced them to her friends, brought them to hear me preach, and included them in the normal course of her life.

They both finally came to faith as a result of two decades of her living out her Christian life before them, combined with helping them through great physical crises. Christie's testimony parallels the importunate widow of Luke 18; she persevered, kept on knocking, and finally the Lord opened the door. But it definitely was not in her timing.

Lesson #3: Pray for others to serve as sources of Christian influence. Sometimes, relatives have a difficult time listening to us. Our parents see us as young and inexperienced about life. Christie's parents didn't understand her faith; they feared the intensity of her commitment to Christ. I had a hard time witnessing to my brother and sister because they knew firsthand the imperfections in my witness. Family members who see our faith sometimes resist talking about their own potential spiritual interests because they fear we'll put too much pressure on them to become like us.

So we pray that God will bring other Christians into the lives of our relatives. My brother's girlfriend (who later became his wife) came into our family life after they met in a bar. They partied together, rode their Harleys together, and lived a fairly wild life. But God used her to bring spirituality into the marriage. Her initial spiritual interest focused on the occult and the spiritual dark side (they even got married on Halloween). But this spiritual attraction got her interested in issues of faith. One Sunday several years ago, they went together to a country church where her distant cousins were singing in a gospel group. When the invitation for salvation was given, she — to my brother's surprise — went forward to receive Christ!

When Christie's brother, a dentist, was acutely lonely because of an isolated job assignment with the U.S. Public Health Service, we prayed that God would bring Christians into his life. He met a fellow dentist, a solid Christian, who befriended him, explained his testimony to him, and invited him to church. Although Christie had the privilege of leading her brother to Christ in prayer, this dentist planted and cultivated seeds that we couldn't.

Lesson #4: Pray for opportunities to demonstrate love, not pressure. We've found that pressing family members for decisions often causes them to react or grow defensive. In the past, when they expressed a spiritual interest or curiosity, we typically reacted with great zeal. Our enthusiasm often caused them to recoil, and they retracted their interest. Why? Perhaps they felt they weren't ready to be as "into" faith as we are. Perhaps they felt pressured.

Christie's mom and dad attended a Billy Graham Crusade with us almost twenty years ago. Her dad seemed spiritually soft that evening. When the invitation was given, he actually went forward to inquire. We praised God, but we weren't quite sure what it meant. We took him out to breakfast, gave him some literature, and really wanted to push him along in his faith. The local crusade organization was also zealous to follow up with him. They sent literature and contacted a local religious leader from his neighborhood church. But this religious leader ridiculed him for having found a "new religion." As a result, our enthusiasm combined with this ridicule actually pushed him away from the faith.

As we evaluate things now, we realize that Christie's mom and dad finally responded to Christ because of the faithful love that they experienced through her — a life of demonstrated love culminated in the latter years of their lives, when she devoted energy and time to their physical care. They responded to the love of Christ that they experienced in her.

Demonstrated love influenced our family members in a second way. We kept them informed about our practical service projects in missions. At times, we even got them involved. This allowed them to express faith on a level they were comfortable with. It also showed them the realness of our Christian faith. This especially influenced Christie's family—whose religious background gave them a tremendous respect for anyone who served the poor. Our involvement with ministries of compassion to the poor served to attract them to our faith.

Lesson #5: Don't lose heart. Luke 18 begins with the explanation that Jesus "[taught] them a parable to show that at all times they ought to pray and not to lose heart" (verse 1, NASB). The implication? It's easy to "lose heart" when our prayers aren't answered as we'd desire. Jesus wants us to persevere, and indeed he rewards such perseverance.

The story of Christie's dad illustrates vividly the need to persevere. With the exception of the "Billy Graham Crusade moment," he seldom expressed spiritual interest. He even aggressively resisted Christian faith for years, citing the hypocrisies of Christians and the hard-to-believe content of the Bible.

On one occasion, we talked through the "bad news" aspect of the good news—that people without Christ go to hell. He resisted this message so strongly that he retorted, "If there's a God who allows people to go to hell, then I don't want to go to heaven to live with him. I choose hell."

A few years later, after the sudden death of his forty-seven-year-old son, her dad again reacted belligerently. When we asked if he would like to receive God's gift of eternal life, he snapped back, "Eternal life is a myth; there's no heaven or hell. Just put me in the grave. The grave is all there is."

This belligerent response made me lose heart. I said, "Let's quit, shake the dust off our feet, and move on." But Christie kept praying—tenaciously. Like the importunate widow, she kept pounding on heaven's door on her father's behalf. We called friends and asked them to join us in prayer for him. We marshaled the prayers of more than five hundred friends and associates (using e-mail), asking them to join us in prayer for his salvation.

Two weeks later, her dad's heart softened. He indicated an interest in coming into a relationship with God. We invited him to pray a simple prayer, and he responded. For the first time in our lives, we heard him pray, "Jesus, have mercy on my soul." His countenance changed. His striving was over. As we stood there hearing this simple prayer for mercy, it was hard to believe that God had finally answered Christie's prayers of twenty-nine years!

Her dad died two weeks later. Christie didn't lose heart in her prayers, and God opened the door of heaven for him.

CONCLUSION

After we come into a relationship with God through Jesus Christ, our first desire is to see our family members share with us in spiritual life. But we've learned that every person's spiritual pilgrimage is unique. People don't come to Christ at the same speed. Their journeys are their journeys, and it often takes awhile. God calls us to stay consistent and involved in their lives. We continue to give them opportunities, but most of all we don't close the door of relationship. And we pray—allowing God to bring the results in his time.

Where do the effects of our persevering prayer and the providence of God intersect? We don't know. God doesn't tell us. He only commands us to pray without ceasing—and our family members are where we start.[1]

SPEAKING
THE SAME LANGUAGE

More Questions to Ask Unbelievers
to Build Understanding

As an evangelical, I've been trained to tell others the good news about Jesus. That's what we evangelicals do best—we tell; we preach; we proclaim. But lately I'm learning to listen.

I swim with a group of guys in our town's version of the YMCA. The same five or six of us show up at least three days per week around noontime for a swimming workout of forty to forty-five minutes. We call ourselves the "Noon Platoon." These guys have become my friends, but my proclamation of the gospel to them has come slowly—mostly because I'm learning to listen.

None of these men go to church. A few have religious upbringings, but most haven't entered a church since about age twelve—except for weddings, funerals, and a Christmas or two. As our relationship has grown, I've discovered my own need to understand their perspectives, beliefs, and worldviews before I attempt to address the gospel to them. In the words of *The Seven Habits of Highly Effective People,* I'm trying "first to understand, then to be understood."[1]

To foster understanding, I invite various Noon Platoon members out to breakfast or lunch. I'm up-front about my motives. I explain, "I work in a religious world where we use phrases and ideas that I'm not sure most people understand. I'd like to take you out for a meal just to ask questions, throw terms at you, and invite your feedback. I just want to understand what you think. And I'll treat!"

A few have joined me, and they tease each other on subsequent days in the locker room for passing or failing "Paul's religious exam." Friendly mocking notwithstanding, I've found great receptivity. And I've learned a lot about my friends and their perceptions about Christian faith. I'm now praying that God will use this understanding to increase my effectiveness as a witness to them and others.

MY QUESTIONS

My questions vary according to the individual and what I might know of his background. I usually keep the questions in four specific categories, and I record his answers—as if I'm taking a survey. I started asking them of my Noon Platoon buddies, but now I take them with me whenever I'm trying to move a conversation in a spiritual direction.

Question #1: Biblical. I often start with some general Bible knowledge, just to see what the person knows.

- "Do you know who came first—Moses, Abraham, Adam, or Jesus?" Most of my friends don't, although they guess that Adam was first.
- "What are the four 'Gospels'?" My swimming partners who went through catechism as children generally get at least two correct. One guy seated next to me on the plane listed "John, Paul, George, and Ringo."
- "What is the Trinity?" One guy answered, "A college in Hartford, Connecticut." I gave him partial credit.

To bring biblical knowledge closer to home, I often ask about the person we see at TV sporting events—on the sidelines or in the end zone at American football games—holding up that huge "John 3:16" sign. I ask if they've ever seen it. All have. Then I ask, "Do you know what it means?" A few knew it is reference to a Bible verse, but had no idea what the verse said.

On this question, one fellow drew a complete blank. I told him it was a verse in the Bible. He responded, "Like something in the Psalms?" His reply assured me that my presentation of the gospel couldn't be built on assumptions about biblical knowledge.

Question #2: Vocabulary. I'm convinced that I often fail as an evangelist because I'm speaking to people in evangelical code-words that church people use, but unchurched people don't understand.

"What does 'eternal life' mean?" Most of my friends seem to believe that the human spirit lives on forever, although none have introduced anything close to the idea of hell—except as a place for *really* bad people like Hitler or Stalin. Even one Jewish fellow, when I explained to him that his own Jewish faith generally didn't teach a concept akin to the Christian "eternal life," said: "Doesn't matter. I still believe in it."

"You're in a church service and the preacher refers to the 'Lamb of God.' What does he mean?" One guy responded, "I'd be lost. I assume it's some type of metaphor, but I have no idea what it means." Based on his reply, I'm giving him a briefing before we go together to the Easter service.

"When you hear a Christian say, 'Jesus died for my sins,' what does it mean?" One former churchgoer said, "I've heard that. I think it has something to do with Jesus' death on the cross." He stood alone in his understanding—at least in my swim group.

"Would you ever use the word 'sin' in your vocabulary?" A lawyer in our group answered smugly, "Yes—as in 'sinfully delicious chocolate.'" "Okay," I replied, "a kid goes to the high school and shoots fifteen of his classmates; would you call that 'sin'?" He said, "I'd call it wrong." I came back, "Based on what?" This provoked some healthy discussion where he admitted that his relativistic worldview contained no basis for judging right and wrong.

"If someone says that he or she has a 'personal relationship with God,' *what do you think it means?"* One man said, "I think it has something to do with intimacy, but the phrase has no meaning to me."

My informal research confirmed what I thought. My friends' answers have caused me to rethink my words, phrases, and evangelical slogans. I'm working harder to communicate Christ to my friends in terms they understand.

Question #3: Sociological and relational. Questions in this category help me discover the person's relationships with or knowledge of other Christians. I'll ask questions about Christians in the news, the faith expressed by public figures like politicians or athletes, or their opinions about issues Christians identify themselves with.

Often I find that a friend has a born-again cousin or in-law. One conversation, however, got completely derailed talking about a wacko aunt who had moved to the mountains to stockpile food, awaiting Y2K and the end of the world—which only serves to illustrate that attempting to listen is not foolproof.

In one conversation with a friend educated at Harvard University, I asked, "What does the term 'evangelical' mean?" It was the only time in the conversation that my friend got animated. He replied, "Evangelicals are the people who are always *against* something. Evangelicals are people who refuse to think. Someone else—or God— tells them what to think."

Unfazed by his reply, I came back, "What makes you think of evangelicals in that way?" He replied, "The way that evangelicals get portrayed in the media," and he referred to recent violence at a local abortion clinic. He also thought that the syrupy religious character Ned Flanders on *The Simpsons* represented evangelicals.

"What about Christie and me—since we're the only evangelicals you actually know?"

"You're okay. Maybe evangelicals just get bad press." This man probably won't come with me to hear an evangelical speaker, but he does listen to us. We invited him and his wife to dinner.

Question #4: Personal spiritual perspective. If the discussion progresses, and I sense my friend is comfortable to answer some "What do *you* really think?" questions, I probe a little more personally.

"You have children. What—if anything—are you teaching them about God?" Most parents I talk with want their children to have some type of religious or moral education. The children may be the reason they start attending church.

"If you could ask God any question, what would it be?" Most reply with questions about pain and suffering in the world. But for one of my friends, this question opened up his greatest pain. He replied, "I'd ask God why he let my ten-year-old son die in a hockey accident." I offered no explanation, but the answer revealed why this guy was the most sarcastic toward all things Christian.

"Where will you go when you die?" The consistency of the answers I get to this question amazes me. All believe they are "going to heaven," "going to a better place," or "on to eternal life." Even a self-confessed atheist replied, "Heaven!" When I follow up with "How do you know?" the consistent reply comes back, "Well, I'm better than most people." The replies to the eternity question has me wondering, "Do I need to tell people the bad news—that they're *not* going to heaven—before I tell them the good news—that Jesus offers the gift of eternal life?"

"How would you classify yourself?" Perhaps the most revealing question and answer comes when I've stated, "In my church world, we tend to classify people as either 'believers' (that is, part of the Christian community) or 'seekers' (that is, on a search for spirituality and a relationship with God). How would you classify yourself—in terms of your own spirituality?"

Get ready for honesty. One fellow simply stated, "Classify me as 'nonreligious.' I'm definitely not a seeker. As far as I can tell, I never think about God." The man whose ten-year-old son died said, "Put me in the 'angry' category." A third fellow said, "Is there a classification for 'religiously ignorant'?"

THE REWARDS OF LISTENING

My questions to my swimming friends have paid off. I'm learning how to be a more effective communicator—in terms that my nonChristian friends understand. These exercises have taught me to look for handles to introduce a Christian perspective, even if I don't get to present the whole gospel message. I've awakened to the reality of secularized people, and I'm praying for wisdom to know how to create spiritual hunger in someone who calls himself nonreligious.

Best of all, listening has opened the doors to speak. In several conversations, my questions about eternal life or a personal relationship with God has resulted in an opportunity to explain my answer to the same question.

But for now, I mostly keep on listening and keep on praying so that I can effectively communicate the love of Christ to the Noon Platoon.[2]

NOTES

HEART BUILDER #1

1. *Webster's Seventh New Collegiate Dictionary* (Springfield, Mass.: G & C Merriam Co., 1971), p. 616.
2. Quoted in Gary Inrig, *A Call to Excellence* (Wheaton, Ill.: Victor Books, 1985), p. 51.
3. Michael Bamberger, Don Yaeger, "Over the Edge," *Sports Illustrated* (April 14, 1997), pp. 60-68.
4. Jon Thompson, "King of Fibers," *National Geographic* (June 1994), pp. 60-78.
5. John Bunyan, *Pilgrim's Progress*, (Chicago, Ill.: Moody Press, n.d.), p. 8.
6. This and the other chapter-closing "sidebars" first appeared in my bimonthly columns for the "Effective Outreach" department of *Rev.* magazine (Loveland, Colo.: Group Publishing, Inc).

HEART BUILDER #2

1. The Daily Bible Study Series, *The Letter to the Romans* (Philadelphia, Penn.: Westminster Press, 1975), p. 18.
2. Quoted in Gordon S. Jackson, *Quotes for the Journey, Wisdom for the Way* (Colorado Springs, Colo.: NavPress, 2000), p. 49.
3. Norman Grubb, *C. T. Studd* (Fort Washington, Penn.: Christian Literature Crusade, 1983), p. 14.
4. Grubb, p. 33.
5. Grubb, p. 179.
6. Louis Paul Lehman, "Sinners Day" (recording) (Waco, Tex.: Word Records, n.d.).
7. John White, *Daring to Draw Near* (Downers Grove, Ill.: InterVarsity, 1977), p. 44.
8. John Stott and David Edwards, *Evangelical Essentials* (Downers Grove, Ill.: InterVarsity, 1988), p. 312.
9. Grubb, p. 54.
10. Ajith Fernando, *Crucial Questions About Hell* (London: Kingsway, 1991), p. 150.
11. Although this is not a direct quote, it is a conclusion reached through a summary of C. S. Lewis in *Mere Christianity* (New York: Macmillan, 1972), p. 66.
12. Fernando, p. 134.
13. Quoted in the "News" section of *Christianity Today*, 16 June 1997, p. 22.
14. Quoted in Fernando, p. 134.
15. Fernando, p. 134.
16. Norman Geisler, "Everything You Wanted to Know About Heaven but Were Afraid to Ask," *Discipleship Journal*, no. 87, 1995, p. 32.
17. This quotation is attributed to Oswald J. Smith, founding pastor of The People's Church in Toronto. For years, it adorned the sanctuary of that church. Smith dedicated his ministry to global missions, and frequently cited this statement as

an incentive to his congregation to keep taking the gospel to people who otherwise wouldn't have a chance to respond.

18. Bryant Myers, in *The New Context of World Mission* (Monrovia, Calif.: MARC, 1996) estimates that our world today contains 1.2 billion practicing Muslims, more than 1 billion who are Buddhist or who practice traditional Chinese religion, and nearly 900 million Hindus. For specific and updated statistics, consult Patrick Johnstone's *Operation World* (London: Paternoster, 2001); and David Barrett, George Kurian, and Todd Johnston, eds., *World Christian Encyclopedia* (London: Oxford Press, 2001).

HEART BUILDER #3

1. Quoted in George Hunter III, *How to Reach Secular People* (Nashville, Tenn.: Abingdon, 1992), p. 112.
2. Hunter, p. 48.
3. Bob Lupton, *Urban Perspectives* newsletter (Atlanta, Ga.: FCS Urban Ministries), Fall 1994.
4. Source unknown.
5. Patrick Johnstone, *Operation World* (Grand Rapids, Mich.: Zondervan, 1993), p. 27. See also *The 10/40 Window: Getting to the Core of the Core* (Colorado Springs, Colo.: The AD2000 Movement, n.d.).
6. Bryant Myers, *The New Context of World Mission* (Monrovia, Calif.: MARC, 1996), pp. 16-20.

HEART BUILDER #4

1. Quoted in Gordon S. Jackson, *Quotes for the Journey, Wisdom for the Way* (Colorado Springs, Colo.: NavPress, 2000), p. 48.
2. The source for this was a baptismal testimony written for a Grace Chapel "new members" class. The name is changed to protect the person. Printed with permission.
3. George Hunter III, *How to Reach Secular People* (Nashville, Tenn.: Abingdon, 1992), p. 32.
4. The "Transferable Concepts" of Campus Crusade for Christ can be ordered through the organization's Web site (www.ccci.org) or through www.transferableconcepts.com.
5. Another of Oswald J. Smith's well-known quotations; see chapter 2, endnote 16.

HEART BUILDER #5

1. Tim Downs, *Finding Common Ground: Communicating with Those Outside the Christian Community* (Chicago, Ill.: Moody, 1999), p. 16.
2. The source for this was a baptismal testimony written for a Grace Chapel "new members" class. The name is changed to protect the person. Printed with permission.
3. Although the thoughts that follow are mine, I am indebted to George Hunter III and his book *How to Reach Secular People* (Nashville, Tenn.: Abingdon, 1992), pp. 44-54, for outlining these ten characteristics.

4. Quoted in Gordon S. Jackson, *Quotes for the Journey, Wisdom for the Way* (Colorado Springs, Colo.: NavPress, 2000), p. 47.

5. From the unpublished manuscript by George Hunter III, "Informing Apostolic Ministry: Research and Writing for Effective Evangelism," an address for the Fall 1999 meeting of the Academy for Evangelism in Theological Education, p. 5.

HEART BUILDER #6

1. Mark Acuff, "Lost and Found: Making Evangelism a Priority," *Ockenga Connections*, vol. 5, no. 2, Summer 2000, p. 1.

HEART BUILDER #7

1. Presented at a seminar on evangelism at Grace Chapel, Lexington, Mass., by Dr. Jerry White, President of The Navigators, September 12, 1989.

2. Mack Stiles, "The Surprising Rewards of Witnessing," *Discipleship Journal*, Issue 119, September/October 2000, p. 74.

3. Howard Snyder, *Liberating the Church* (Downers Grove, Ill.: InterVarsity, 1983), p. 11.

4. Quoted in Gordon S. Jackson, *Quotes for the Journey, Wisdom for the Way* (Colorado Springs, Colo.: NavPress, 2000), p. 49.

5. Bill Hybels and Mark Mittelburg, *Becoming a Contagious Christian* (Grand Rapids, Mich.: Zondervan, 1994), pp. 40-ff.

6. Quoted in Jackson, p. 46.

7. While the descriptions that follow are mine, I owe the three "posture" ideas to Dick Staub and his article, "Please Pass the Salt," *Discipleship Journal*, Issue 122, March/April 2001, p. 42.

8. Dean Merrill, *Sinners in the Hands of an Angry Church* (Grand Rapids, Mich.: Zondervan, 1997), pp. 48-52.

9. Leith Anderson, *Leadership That Works* (Minneapolis, Minn.: Bethany House, 1999), p. 135.

10. Lesslie Newbegin, *The Gospel in a Pluralistic Society* (Grand Rapids, Mich.: Eerdmans, 1989), p. 101.

11. Newbegin, p. 232.

12. Vincent Donovan, *Christianity Rediscovered* (Maryknoll, N.Y.: Orbis, 1978), p. 78.

13. Personal conversation with Zac Niringiye on December 29, 1991.

HEART BUILDER #8

1. Mark Acuff, "Lost and Found: Making Evangelism a Priority," *Ockenga Connections*, vol. 5, no. 2, Summer 2000, p. 1.

2. These five ideas first appeared in my book *Six Dangerous Questions to Transform Your Worldview* (Downers Grove, Ill.: InterVarsity, 1996), pp. 100-108.

3. F. F. Bruce, *Tyndale New Testament Commentary, Romans* (Grand Rapids, Mich.: Eerdmans, 1978), p. 205.

4. Ruth Tucker, *From Jerusalem to Irian Jaya* (Grand Rapids, Mich.: Zondervan, 1983), p. 115.

HEART BUILDER #9

1. Tim Muehlhoff, "Can You Relate?" *Discipleship Journal*, Issue 122, March/April 2001, p. 60.
2. Dick Staub, "Please Pass the Salt," *Discipleship Journal*, Issue 122, March/April 2001, p. 44.
3. Quoted in Gordon S. Jackson, *Quotes for the Journey, Wisdom for the Way* (Colorado Springs, Colo.: NavPress, 2000), p. 50.
4. Quoted in Jackson, p. 46.
5. For more information, write to Evangelicals for Social Action, 10 East Lancaster Avenue, Wynnewood, PA 19096.
6. Dick Staub, "Following Jesus to the Party," *PRISM*, November/December 2000, p. 9.
7. Mark Acuff, "Lost and Found: Making Evangelism a Priority," *Ockenga Connections*, vol. 5, no. 2, Summer 2000, p. 2.
8. George G. Hunter III, "Informing Apostolic Ministry: Research and Writing for Effective Evangelism," an address for the Fall 1999 meeting of the Academy for Evangelism in Theological Education, p. 6.

THE END RESULT

1. Mack Stiles, "The Surprising Rewards of Witnessing," *Discipleship Journal*, Issue 119, September/October 2000, p. 74.

APPENDIX A

1. Appendix A first appeared in *Discipleship Journal*, Issue 126, November/December 2001, pp. 28-32.

APPENDIX B

1. Steven Covey, *The Seven Habits of Highly Effective People* (New York: Simon and Schuster, 1989), p. 235.
2. Appendix B first appeared in *Discipleship Journal*, Issue 127, January/February 2002, p. 27.

PAUL BORTHWICK dedicates himself to mobilizing others for outreach and missions. He served twenty-two years as youth pastor, then missions pastor, on the staff of Grace Chapel in Lexington, Massachusetts. He is now senior consultant for the leadership development ministry Development Associates International.

Paul and his wife, Christie, have coordinated one hundred cross-cultural service teams for youth and adults, been involved in the Urbana Student Mission Convention, and traveled to encourage Christian workers around the world. He is the author of more than ten books and a variety of articles on topics related to missions, leadership, discipleship, and youth. Paul and Christie live in Lexington.

DEVELOP AN EVANGELISTIC MINDSET.

Divine Appointments

Divine appointments rarely take place in ideal
environments. This book will show you how to leave the
"holy huddle" and enter the world of unbelievers with
the prayer: "Lord, open my eyes today to a person
who needs to know You."
By Bob Jacks, Matthew Jacks, and Pam Mellskog

101 Ways to Reach Your Community

You don't have to be gifted in evangelism to successfully
share your faith. Here are 101 simple, effective ways
to demonstrate the love of God and win a
hearing for the gospel.
By Steve Sjogren

A Mind for Missions

Ten building blocks for seeing the world beyond our
borders—a world full of people that need God's love
and our love.
By Paul Borthwick

To get your copies, visit your local bookstore, call 1-800-366-7788, or log
on to www.navpress.com. Ask for a FREE catalog of NavPress products.
Offer #BPA.

NAVPRESS
BRINGING TRUTH TO LIFE
www.navpress.com